HANDBOOK FOR
NEW CATHOLICS

HANDBOOK for NEW CATHOLICS

By

Aloysius J. Burggraff, C.S.P., Ph.D.
Director, Catholic Information Center, Baltimore, Md.

Paulist Press
(Paulist Fathers)
New York, N. Y.

FOREWORD

CONVERTS, especially new ones, frequently find themselves buried in the details of external ritual. There are so many things to learn. Trying to carry out the letter of the law seems to kill the spirit of devotion. There is the fear of making mistakes and becoming a spectacle to others. The various externals of worship, instead of being a stepping stone to the great invisible realities, become a stumbling block.

No instructor could anticipate all the problems that a convert will meet in practicing the Faith. Even many of the things he did say are soon forgotten. No two converts meet with the same problems. As in the case of swimming, one must learn by doing.

It is the purpose of this handbook of Catholic practices to simplify things for beginners in the Catholic Faith by giving a few "ground rules" and at the same time providing an easy reference book for learning various details of Catholic practices.

May this booklet be your daily companion to guide you on your journey into the rich consolations of the Catholic Faith.

A. J. BURGGRAFF, C.S.P.

CONTENTS

Foreword 5

I. The Church Calendar 9

II. Assisting at Mass 13

III. Reception of the Sacraments.... 43

IV. A Catholic Prays 73

V. Devotions 85

VI. Sacramentals 105

VII. Fasting and Abstinence........ 117

VIII. Lent and Holy Week.......... 125

IX. Blessings 131

X. Christian Symbols 137

XI. Indulgences, Retreats, Stipends. 147

XII. How To. 153

XIII. Supplementary Reading 159

XIV. Forms of Address 165

XV. Baptismal Names for Boys and
Girls 169

Index 179

I
THE
CHURCH
CALENDAR

IN HER LITURGICAL SERVICES, the Church
commemorates annually the main events in
the life of our Lord and Savior, Jesus Christ.
These events are celebrated, not as mere
historical facts, but as a reliving of these
facts in the liturgy of the Church. And the
faithful observe these events, not as spectators, but as participants. The liturgical
year or cycle is centered about two main
events in the Savior's life, His birth and His
resurrection. It begins with the birth of our
Savior.

Advent, the period of anticipation, of ex-
pectation of the Savior, begins with the
Sunday nearest to the feast of St. Andrew,
November 30. The first Sunday of Advent
is the first day of the New Year in the
Church calendar. Since the season of Advent
is one of preparation and penance, looking

forward in a spirit of temperance and mortification, the liturgical color is purple; hence purple vestments at Mass; subdued or no organ music during Mass; no flowers for decoration on the altar. December 24, the vigil of the birth of the Savior, ends the season of Advent.

The date of Easter, commemorating the resurrection of our Savior, is the first Sunday after the full moon which occurs on or after March 21, the vernal or spring equinox. Prior to Easter is the 40-day (Latin, *quadragesima*) period of penance called Lent. The first Sunday of Lent is called *Quadragesima* Sunday. Lent, a season of penance, is dedicated to the memory of our Lord's passion and death. In the early Church, the season of penance lasted for 70 days (Latin, *septuagesima*) and is still penitential in the spirit of the liturgy. It is called the Septuagesima period, beginning three weeks before Lent on Septuagesima Sunday.

The Easter season solemnity is extended fifty (Latin, *pente*) days, ending with Pentecost Sunday. In spirit the entire period is observed as the paschal season. The period from Pentecost to Advent is designated as "after Pentecost," and the Sundays are numbered Sundays after Pentecost. This season is one of hope, looking forward to the coming of the Savior. The color of hope is green.

All feast days of the Church calendar which are reckoned from Easter we call the movable feast days — they move or change with the date of Easter. Some feast days are celebrated on the same date each year and are called "fixed feasts."

The fixed feast days on which we are bound to attend Mass are:

> Christmas, December 25
> Circumcision, January 1
> Ascension of Our Lord, 40 days after Easter
> Assumption of Mary, August 15
> All Saints, November 1
> Immaculate Conception, December 8

II
ASSISTING
AT
MASS

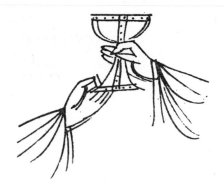

THE MASS is magnificent because it is the most perfect act of worship that man could possibly offer God. However, it is by no means the simplest. Only study and reflection can even begin to reveal the profound truths and spiritual fruits of the Mass, which is the renewal of the divine drama of salvation enacted at the Last Supper and on Calvary. Converts, especially, must be warned not to be discouraged if at first they get little visible results out of the Mass even after putting much into it. It will grow in appreciation and bear more fruit with study and time. Because the Mass is such a perfect act of worship, however profound, space is devoted to explain some of the elementary and underlying principles, with the hope that even new Catholics will be able to participate in the spirit and fruits of the Mass without being buried in a maze of details. This is meant to be just the scaffold that will enable a beginner to form a way of worship that will mirror the magnificence of the Mass.

The Perfect Way of Worship

IN HUMAN relations, true love ends in *worship* of the beloved. The problem is how to express to another, one's inner devotion of heart and mind. Words are something. When words fail, music. But the perfect visible expression of love is gift-giving. The more precious the gift, the more satisfied is the inner instinct of love, which wants to reach into infinity. Only the gift made precious and sacred through sacrifice comes nearest to satisfying our feeling of true love for another.

From the beginning man adored God by gift-giving. The Bible opens with Cain and Abel worshiping by offering gifts. It satisfied a deep human instinct, especially if the gift pleased God. God is pleased with sacrifice when and because it visibly measures for man himself, man's love and adoration for God. God, who knows the very thoughts and intents of the heart needs no instruction, no demonstration.

The disposition of the heart with which the gift is offered is even more important than the gift itself. Abel offered "the firstlings of his flock." And the Lord was pleased with Abel and his offerings. Cain also offered fruits of the earth, but God was not pleased with Cain and his offerings, for his offerings were made with an evil heart. Two elements, especially, have made man's offering acceptable to God:

1. The purpose—to adore and to serve God.

2. Man's sincerity—to test man's willingness to surrender the gift to God.

As in human love, so in adoration of God, no gift seems precious enough to express love worthy of the Infinite. The best does not seem good enough. There is one gift which is magnificent, perfect, and that is the sacrifice of our Savior to His Father in heaven. Since Christ was both man and God, the sacrifice of the human nature of Christ, to the extent of life itself, was glorified, made infinite by being offered through His divine will and personality. Here is the one gift worthy of God's love for man and a gift whereby man can express his love worthy of God. For, indeed, this is precisely man's opportunity.

By means of the Last Supper, the Savior arranged that His supreme sacrifice on the Cross could be re-enacted, in an unbloody manner, but no less real and precious. He put into the hands of men—when He commanded His apostles to do this in commemoration of Him, i.e., His death—the possibility and opportunity of offering a perfect Gift to God. Through the separate changing, consecration, of the bread and the wine, man "shows forth the death of the Lord." And because Christ, the Victim, the same who offered Himself on Calvary, is really present as He was on Calvary, the Mass is of infinite spiritual value.

A principal fruit (grace) of the sacrifice of the Mass is the Eucharist, which we receive in holy communion. Hence through the sacrifice of the Mass, man offers the perfect gift of love to God. In the sacrament of holy communion, God gives Himself to man.

The union between our human nature and God, while not in the degree to which the human nature of Christ and His divine nature were united, nevertheless, is something more than that of being in the state of grace. It is a personal union with Christ, something not to be measured in sentiment or emotional love as in the case of our fellow man. It is beyond the reach of our feelings. It can be measured by the price that was paid to make it possible, the very life of the God-Man, Jesus Christ, our Savior. This is why the Mass was meant to do something more than provide us with holy communion. "Do this in remembrance of Me," of My love measured by My gift, the gift of life itself. First commemorate My death on the cross and then participate in the graces merited by My sacrifice in receiving holy communion. If one would know what it means to commune with God and thus save his soul, let him contemplate the crucifix.

How to Assist at Mass

THIS IS for the new Catholic a challenge and an opportunity. It is a challenge because in his non-Catholic services, he had a personal part, both in the prayers and the music. Now, he may find himself in a parish that has not as yet introduced the practice of the laity's outward participation — with responses and singing—in the Holy Sacrifice of the Mass. Therefore, the Mass, especially a low Mass, will seem somewhat cold and formal. Let him recall what was said about gift-giving as the more perfect way of expressing love; and how the sacrifice of the Mass is the one perfect, magnificent way.

Although it is necessary in the case of the Holy Sacrifice of the Mass, that the one offering it be an ordained man, the congregation is not, must not be, mere spectators. The people are participants, in fact, offer the gift to God through the consecrated hands of the priest. The extent to which each person shares in the fruits of the Mass depends much on the closeness of the person's participation in the Mass and the person's own interior disposition. The ideal, liturgical, although not the simplest way to assist at Mass is to pray the Mass rather than say prayers during the Mass. By means of a missal the lay person can say the prayers of the Mass; he is encouraged to sing the Mass in case of a sung Mass. Much effort has been made recently to encourage and aid the lay person in participating in the Mass. Here is the problem, especially for beginners: "how to keep up with the priest." For this purpose, we make the following suggestions and give an audio-visual outline of the Mass:

1. Use a missal, if only for reference, with the outline suggested.
2. It is not necessary to say all the prayers in order to assist at Mass.

3. Better to say some of the prayers devoutly than to race through all of them.

4. Make the thought of the prayer your own even though another composed the words.

5. Start by following the Ordinary (the unchanged part) of the Mass; in due time you can work in the proper parts (the parts of the Mass that change each day).

It is sufficient, but important, that we have a general but correct understanding of the parts of the Mass and have some "shorthand" way of recognizing the part the priest may be saying at a given time. For this purpose, we give the following outline of the Mass, designating the steps of each part by visual aids, i.e., position of hands, the head, even the body, of the celebrant, visual aids that will not only "tell where the priest is" but be symbolic of the words being said. By using the missal as a reference, the person will be able to add the prayers and eventually say all of them.

The sacrifice of the Mass is expressed in both words and actions—the latter are easier to grasp; the former are not necessary for an elementary appreciation and participation in the Mass. We pray with our tongue, our hands, our head, our whole body; kneeling, standing, sitting, all have their symbolic meaning declaring the inner disposition of the mind and heart. Raising of the head, eyes and hands mean adoration; bowing of head and striking of the breast means contrition. The priest praying with outstretched hands usually signifies the offering of the prayers of the congregation to God; praying with hands folded means asking God's blessing and forgiveness of the people.

Outline of the Mass

I. The Foremass (Preparation)

MAN'S PRAYERS ASCEND TO GOD	Prayers of Preparation Gloria Collect
GOD'S INSTRUCTIONS TO MAN	Epistle Gospel Sermon Creed

II. The Sacrifice

WE BRING AND OFFER OUR GIFT	Offertory Consecration
WE RECEIVE GOD'S GIFT	Communion

VISUAL PRESENTATION
OF
PARTS OF THE MASS

I. THE FOREMASS

PRAYERS OF PREPARATION
Through My Fault
Cleansing of Heart and Mind

INTROIT
Introduction
Key to the Proper of the Mass

GLORIA
"Glory to God"
(Omitted when color of vestments is purple or black)

23

THE COLLECT
Offering of Mind and Heart to God

THE GOSPEL
"Cleanse my mind, lips and heart that I may worthily
read the Holy Gospel."

THE CREED
"I believe in God . . ."

BEGINNING THE SACRIFICE OF THE MASS

THE OFFERTORY

DOMINUS VOBISCUM
"The Lord be with you."

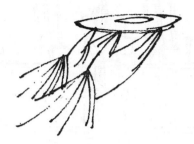

OFFERING GIFTS (Bread)
"Accept, O Holy Father, this spotless host."

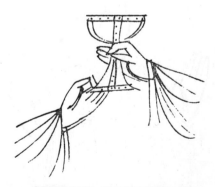

OFFERING GIFTS (Wine)
"We offer You, O Lord, the chalice of salvation."

THE LAVABO
"I will wash my hands among the innocent."
Spiritual Purification

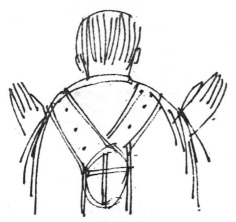

PREFACE
Sursum Corda
"Lift up your Hearts"

THE SANCTUS
"Blessed is He who comes"

THE CANON

MEMENTO OF THE LIVING
"Be mindful, O Lord"
(*Not Illustrated*)

BEFORE THE CONSECRATION
Hanc Igitur
"Receive in atonement"

CONSECRATION

You Offer God's Gift to Him
"Showing forth the death of the Lord"

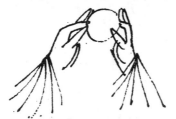

ELEVATION OF HOST
"This is My Body"

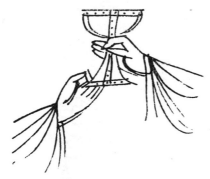

ELEVATION OF THE CHALICE
"This is My Blood"

MEMENTO OF THE DEAD
(*Not Illustrated*)

"Be mindful, O Lord, of Your servants who have
gone before us."

Pater Noster (Said aloud)
"Our Father who art in heaven"

COMMUNION

DOMINE NON SUM DIGNUS
"Lord, I am not worthy"

PRIEST'S COMMUNION

"May the Body of our Lord Jesus Christ keep my
soul unto life everlasting. Amen."

PRIEST CONSUMES PRECIOUS BLOOD

"May the Blood of our Lord Jesus Christ keep my
soul unto life everlasting. Amen."

PEOPLES' COMMUNION

ECCE AGNUS DEI
"Behold the Lamb of God"

THE ABLUTION
"Grant that no trace of sin be found in me"

THE DISMISSAL
"Go, you are dismissed."

THE FINAL BLESSING
"May Almighty God bless you."

The Missal

THE MISSAL used by the priest in saying Mass contains all the prayers, said or recited by the priest in offering the Mass, as well as the directions needed by the priest to exercise his devotion of sacrifice properly. The directions are usually printed in red and are called the rubrics from *rubor,* Latin for red. The missal has been translated into various languages for the use of the laity.

My Sunday Missal contains the prayers for Sunday Masses and holydays only. It has a guide system for the reader which will help him to follow the prayers in the correct order for each Sunday. The missal is divided into two main parts one containing the prayers common to all the Masses, the other those that are special or proper for each Mass. *My Sunday Missal* is recommended for beginners, since it is more simplified in form.

The Daily Missal, like the large missal used by the priest, contains all the Masses of the Church year. It is published in one volume, two volumes, or four volumes corresponding to the four seasons of the year.

The Leaflet Missal contains all the prayers, both proper and common, arranged together to make the reading easier. Each Sunday has a separate leaflet missal. Some churches provide the leaflet missal for the parishioners each Sunday.

Again, the beginner must be encouraged to persevere in using the missal to assist at Mass. Continued use of it will acquaint the reader with its structure and operation. He not only will have the satisfaction of assisting at Mass liturgically, but it will be a real joy to do so. The structure of the Mass on Sundays or weekdays is the same. It is a serious matter to miss Mass deliberately on Sundays and holydays of obligation.

Why Mass on Sunday?

FORMER NON-CATHOLICS who usually went to church when they felt like it find regular attendance at Mass on Sundays difficult to appreciate. It seems to be an arbitrary regulation of the Church. We should go to church because we want to, not because we have to.

To appreciate the obligation of attending Sunday Mass, and under the pain of mortal sin, we must first realize that the time and manner of worship depends not on personal feeling but on divine Law. We love God, not through sporadic rise in human unction, but by the rational act of the will based on an intelligent understanding of the Will of God.

"Remember thou keep holy the Lord's Day." This divine command of God sets a certain time for worship. How to keep the Lord's Day holy is also determined by the Will of God, not the feelings of men. The Church, who knows the Will of God, tells us specifically what we must do to please God— the way of keeping the Lord's Day holy is to assist at the holy sacrifice of the Mass, which is the unbloody re-enaction of the sacrifice of the cross.

Ever since the fall of man, it is not natural for man to be religious. It is a question of will power to do what we ought to when we don't want to. To will to assist at Mass on Sundays, rather than be drawn by some inner unction, is quite the normal, and correct state of religious worship.

Missing Mass

BECAUSE THE Mass is the central feature of the Catholic religion, missing Mass on Sundays deliberately is a mortal sin. One misses Mass if he is deliberately absent from any main part, that is, the Offertory, the Consecration or the Communion.

One is excused from Mass in the case of illness; great distance (over an hour's walk or a 25-mile ride in a car) ; or necessary work at home such as caring for the sick or very young children. Being on vacation is not a bona fide excuse unless permission has been previously obtained from the pastor.

Holydays of Obligation

ON HOLYDAYS Catholics must attend Mass under penalty of mortal sin. The particular days appointed by the bishops of a country vary with the Holy See's approval. In the United States they are:

All Sundays

The Feast of the Circumcision of Our Lord—January 1

The Feast of our Lord's Ascension— Thursday—the 40th day after Easter

The Feast of our Lady's Assumption— August 15

The Feast of All Saints—November 1

The Feast of the Immaculate Conception —December 8

The Feast of our Lord's Birth— December 25

Daily Mass

ALTHOUGH MASS is said daily in most churches several times at various hours for the convenience of the worshipers, there is no obligation to assist at daily Mass. Many converts do so. It seems an added satisfaction to assist at Mass, not because we have to, but because we want to.

The Sacrifice of the Mass illustrates so admirably that love is shown in gift giving. The gift is made more precious when made possible through sacrifice on our part. The effort we make to assist at Mass demonstrates visibly to ourselves how much we appreciate God's gift to us, the sacrifice of His life. "Greater love than this no one has, that one lay down his life for his friends."

A convert who walked six miles to church, when her rider failed to show up, remarked, "Holy Communion never tasted sweeter than that day."

Don't be discouraged or disillusioned if at first you get little visible and tangible satisfaction from assisting at Mass. It is a common experience for new converts to get lost in the details of external ritual of the Mass. Trying to keep to the letter of the liturgy, they lose the spirit of devotion at Mass. The full meaning and glory of the Mass will unfold as you learn more about the substance of the Mass by getting acquainted with the details. Do not worry about making mistakes in your external worship. Although the church be packed, you can make the Mass your Mass and your appreciation of the Mass and participation in it a very personal one.

Types of Masses

Low Mass—A Mass which is read by the celebrant; in part aloud, in part silently.

High Mass—A Mass which is sung by the celebrant and a choir.

Solemn Mass—A high Mass with added externals. Three ministers take part and incense is used. The Gospel is first read by the celebrant and then sung by the deacon.

Nuptial Mass—A Mass said for the bride and groom on their wedding day.

Requiem Mass—A Mass said for the dead. A funeral Mass is a Requiem Mass said usually with the body present.

Rules for the Laity at Low Mass

Stand when priest enters the sanctuary.

Kneel when he begins prayers at foot of the altar.

Stand at beginning of the Gospel and make triple sign of cross with thumb on forehead, lips and breast.

Remain standing for the Creed, if it is said, and *genuflect* when the priest does.

Sit for the Offertory and so remain until Sanctus bells.

Kneel at Sanctus.

Sit after Communion when priest takes water and wine.

Kneel for blessing.

Stand at beginning of Last Gospel. Make triple sign of cross with thumb on forehead, lips and breast, and *genuflect* when priest does.

Kneel for prayers after Mass.

Stand as priest leaves the sanctuary.

Rules for the Laity at High Mass

Stand when procession to altar makes its appearance from sacristy. If *Asperges* takes place (people are sprinkled with holy water) *stand*. Each person *bows* and makes the sign of the cross when sprinkled at the *Asperges*.

Sit during time priest puts on vestments for Mass.

Kneel during prayers at foot of altar. *Stand* when priest ascends steps of altar. If, during the *Kyrie*, the celebrant sits, the people *sit*;

when he rises, the people *stand*. *Sit* with priest during Gloria; *rise* when he does. (In Requiem Mass, *kneel* during singing of prayers.)

Sit while the Epistle is chanted or read.

Stand for the chanting of the Gospel. Make triple sign of the cross with thumb on forehead, lips and breast.

Remain Standing during the Creed, genuflecting when the celebrant genuflects.

Sit when the celebrant sits. *Stand* when the celebrant rises.

At *Dominus Vobiscum,* after Creed, *sit* during the Offertory. (*Stand* during incensation of the people.)

Stand when the celebrant begins to sing (*Per omnia saecula saeculorum*) before beginning the Preface.

Kneel when bell is rung unless the people sing the Sanctus, in which case *stand* until the end of the Sanctus.

During the Consecration, you may *bow*; then raise your eyes in adoration of the Sacred Host as the priest raises It for the faithful to adore. Repeat for the Consecration of the wine.

Stand after the elevation (after chalice is raised by the celebrant). In Requiem Mass —*kneel*.

Sit after celebrant has taken the Precious Blood unless Holy Communion is distributed, in which case, *kneel*. *Sit* when tabernacle door is closed.

Stand when *Dominus Vobiscum* is sung. (In Requiem Mass *kneel* while prayer is sung.)

Kneel when priest gives the blessing, making the sign of the cross.

Stand during reading of the last Gospel, make triple sign of the cross, with thumb on forehead, lips and breast, and genuflect with the priest.

III
RECEPTION
OF THE
SACRAMENTS

BAPTISM is the first sacrament to be received because without it we do not have the capacity to receive any of the other six sacraments. That is why the convert in becoming a Catholic is baptized at least conditionally, if not absolutely. The priest must make certain that the candidate is really baptized, if not in the first baptism which was administered in some non-Catholic church, then certainly in the conditional baptism.

The sacrament of baptism imparts two important elements into the soul of man. It gives supernatural life, that is, sanctifying grace, thus washing away the spiritual emptiness resulting from original sin. In the case of an adult, it also takes away all sin committed before baptism. And it imparts a permanent quality, called character, to the soul. We may lose sanctifying grace, that is, God's friendship, by committing a serious sin; but we do not lose the character of baptism. We may divorce ourselves from God by committing a mortal sin, but God does not withdraw the soul's permanent quality, the character of baptism. Through repentance and pardon, we can be reconciled to God's good graces. Baptism puts God's life into our soul. The other sacraments nourish that life. But first the seed must be planted. Hence the importance of a valid baptism for the convert and the importance of baptizing babies as soon as possible.

Baptism of Infants

CHURCH LAW requires infants to be baptized publicly as soon after birth as health permits. Two to four weeks is a maximum normal period of time. The date and time of the baptism should be arranged with the priest. This solemn baptism must take place in the parish church of the parents unless their pastor gives written permission for the infant to be baptized elsewhere.

The infant's clothes should not be so tight around the neck that they cannot be loosened with ease for the various anointings. The infant's sponsors or godparents are to be practical Catholics, fourteen years of age or older, who will be able to fulfill the obligation of rearing the child in the Catholic Faith if necessity arises.

One sponsor or godparent is necessary for solemn baptism; two, one of each sex, is customary. Neither is to be the parent of the child; nor in the case of an adult, the spouse of the person baptized. A non-Catholic is never permitted to act as sponsor.

Information for the records consists of: Infant's name, date and place of birth and of baptism, father's name and address, mother's maiden name, sponsors' names. A Christian name, that is, the name of a saint, is to be given to the child.[1]

Simple baptism is administered under emergency conditions anywhere. It is absolutely necessary for the person giving the sacrament to:

1. Intend to give the sacrament.

2. Pour water, preferably on the forehead, of the infant or adult being baptized.

3. Say at the same time, "I baptize you in the name of the Father and of the Son and of the Holy Spirit."

---

[1] See list page **169.**

No sponsors are necessary for emergency baptism, though it is advisable to have one. In case of recovery, the infant or adult must be brought to the church in suitable time for the other ceremonies and anointings to be supplied by the priest who can then record all pertinent information in the church's baptismal register. Sponsors may then be present.

Baptismal certificates then or later in life can be obtained from the pastor of the church where the person received the sacrament. If records are kept in a Catholic hospital, the certificate may be obtained there.

CONFESSION often proves to be a stumbling block to new converts. For this reason the practical aspect of making a good confession will be given in some detail. Even those who have no serious sins to confess find the actual confession awkward and a bit unnatural. For those who have some serious sin to confess and conquer, confession may seem next to impossible, partly because they may misunderstand the requirements for a sincere confession. The result is they delay going to confession until they lose courage completely and, not infrequently, join the number of the fallen-away Catholics.

No one will ever get used to going to confession, any more than he ever gets used to going to the dentist. In either case our reason must dictate to our feelings. With the example before us of self-confessed sinners

that became saints, we should take courage
and thank God for the divine institution of
the sacrament of penance.

As the fear of going to confession mounts,
the arguments against the need of it mount
—"Why can't I confess my sins to God directly in the secret of my heart?" You can.
But how can you be certain that you are forgiven? Can you be forgiven at all! What
must I do to atone for my sins? In short,
what must I do to be saved? If it were sufficient for forgiveness to confess sins directly
to God, why did Christ forgive sins over and
over again, and to those who were being
condemned by their own fellow men? Why
did Christ give the authority to His apostles
to forgive sins in His name if one could confess to God directly? "He breathed upon
them, and said to them, 'Receive the Holy
Spirit; whose sins you shall forgive, they are
forgiven them; and whose sins you shall re-
tain, they are retained.'" (*John 20, 22f.*)
After you apologize to someone for having
offended him, you never know whether you
are forgiven until he gives you some *external*
mark of his inner disposition. You cannot
read another's mind—you cannot sense another's heart. Much less can you "feel" you
are forgiven by God.

How could the apostles forgive until they were told what to forgive? The power to forgive presupposes the telling of the sins we want forgiven. Confessing one's sins to one of God's ordained and official representatives as a prerequisite for forgiveness is an historical fact since the first days of Christianity. It certainly would not, in fact, could not, have been invented. Only the fact that confession is a divine institution could justify it in the eyes of men.

People who have sinned grievously often despair of being forgiven. Only the assurance of divine authority as manifested through the sacrament of penance can convince them otherwise.

The confessor who, like the apostles, knows the mind of God and by ordination, has been given the authority to speak in His name, is the official witness to the sinner's apology, which the sinner makes to God. Through the confessor, God's forgiveness and means of reparation are assured. What greater consolation can come to anyone than to a grievous sinner who wants certitude of forgiveness and release from the sense of guilt and an opportunity to make good?

Again, people hesitate to go to confession because they think their sorrow is not sin-

cere. One reason is they don't "feel" sorrowful; for another, they may commit the same
sin again. Sorrow is an act of the will, not a
rise of the emotions. We can be truly sorry
for our sins without any emotional reaction.
Do we regret doing anything against God's
teaching? To admit that anything against
God's commandments is a sin has the element of sorrow for sin in it. Even if we
have not, may not, succeed in conquering
the sin personally but still admit that it is
wrong in principle because it offends against
God's revelation, then we are sorry.

To be genuinely sorry we must include an
amendment of our sinful ways. There must
be an honest resolve to avoid sin in the future
and as far as possible the near or immediate
occasions of sin. A near occasion of sin is
any circumstance which we know, from past
experience, will lead us into sin. A firm purpose of amendment is concerned with the
present. We may suspect that we may fall
again into the same sin in the future. That
does not imply that our amendment is not
firm and sincere here and now. It is the
present moment and our present intention
that counts in confession. Are we honestly
trying to do our best; then our contrition
is sincere. The only sinner who fails is the

sinner who stops trying. Going to confession is like going to school. The ideal is 100. How many get it? But we are expected to try our best. God sees and counts our sincere effort.

The most effective way of conquering the fear of confession is to go soon after our reception into the Church. One should not delay more than a month. New converts should mention to the priest that they are recent converts. The priest will bear with any mistakes and help them to make a good confession.

What to Tell

THERE ARE two things to bear in mind, the kind of sin we have committed and the number of times. Regarding the kind of sin, the first thing to remember is that only mortal sins are a matter of obligation to confess. And secondly, we must mention which commandment we sinned against and any circumstance that may affect the nature of the sin. For example, it is not sufficient to say, "I committed adultery." Are you married or single? Was the other party married? There are several excellent forms of examination of conscience which will guide the penitent in telling any necessary details. We recommend the one given below.

Venial sins may be confessed. Habitual venial sins, such as a habit of uncharitable criticism, should be confessed. However, do not worry about a complete confession of venial sins. That is not necessary for a good confession. All venial sins are forgiven by a sincere act of contrition. It is profitable to mention venial sins, although we are under no obligation to do so. Nothing can give us greater certitude that they are really forgiven. And doing so will be a guard against committing mortal sins. "He who is faithful in that which is least is faithful also in that which is greater." We will receive special graces to avoid those venial sins in the future.

While we are not obliged to mention doubtful mortal sins, for peace of mind, it is best that we do so.

Concerning the number of times we may have committed a sin, it is not necessary to be mathematically exact. God does not require the impossible. An honest estimate is sufficient, i.e., on the average of once or twice a day, or a week, and so forth.

There is only one thing that will cause us to make a bad confession—to omit deliberately mentioning a sin which we are certain is mortal. And until the bad confession is made good by telling the confessor what we omitted, subsequent confessions and communions only add to our sin. A bad confession can be remedied rather easily. Just tell the confessor that you made a bad confession. The confessor, rather than reprimand, will help to right matters by helping you to review your past confessions.

Perhaps the people who find confession the most difficult are those who have "nothing to confess." Souls who would really have nothing to confess are rare. By using an examination of conscience guide, they will find venial sins which they are guilty of. In order to receive absolution validly, they can mention some serious sin of the past. Their confession could go something like this: "Bless me, Father, for I have sinned. My last confession was a week ago. I can't remember having committed any deliberate sins since then. However, I am sorry for any sins I may be unaware of and for the sin of anger (or adultery) which I committed in my past life."

Examination of Conscience

BEFORE EXAMINING your conscience, note the conditions necessary for a sin to be mortal:

1. It must be a serious offense (grave matter) against the law of God.
2. It must be done with sufficient reflection to know it is wrong and to do it deliberately.
3. It must be done with full consent of the will, that is, you were free and willing to do it. Converts may be forced to do something against their will under home conditions.

If any of these three conditions is lacking, the sin is not mortal.

To begin with, we may need a detailed examination of conscience. But in time we learn our usual failures and can limit the examination to a few questions and eliminate the rest. This detailed examination is meant to cover any and all possibilities.

Prayer before Examination of Conscience

O LORD GOD, you enlighten every man who comes into this world; enlighten my heart, I pray You, with the light of Your grace, that I may fully know my sins, shortcomings, and negligences, and may confess them with that true sorrow and contrition of heart which I so much need. I desire to make full amends for all my sins, and to avoid them for the future to Your honor and glory, and to the salvation of my soul, though Jesus Christ our Lord. Amen.

In the following examination of conscience, sins that are definitely mortal in principle are marked (M); those that may be mortal are marked (D) doubtful; those that are venial are marked (V).

If you find that certain things are sinful which you did not realize before, you were not guilty of committing these sins. However, in the future you will be held responsible for such sins.

Detailed Examination of Conscience

How long since my last confession?
Did I deliberately keep back any mortal sin? (M)
Did I forget any mortal sin?
Did I say my penance?

First Commandment

Habitual neglect of daily prayers (V)
Praying habitually without attention (V)
Denying because of shame that I am a Catholic (D)
Deliberately taking part in Protestant worship (M)
Believing seriously in fortune telling (M)

Second Commandment

Profanity (D)
Asking God to damn others (M)
Using God's name irreverently (V)
Taking oaths (attempting a second marriage ceremony) needlessly (M)

Third Commandment

Deliberately (no excuse) missing Mass on Sundays or holydays (M)
Coming late habitually to Mass (D)
Being irreverent at Mass (V)
Doing manual labor without necessity much of the day (M)

Fourth Commandment

Neglecting one's parent in serious need (M)
Neglecting one's duty to children in serious matter (M)
Disobeying legitimate authority (Speeding) (D)

Fifth Commandment

Striking another in anger (D)
Being mean to others (V)
Seriously wishing evil on others (M)
Hating others for period of time (D)
Quarreling habitually (D)
Giving bad example (D)

Getting completely drunk (M)
Planning or attempting to take life (M)

Sixth and Ninth Commandments

Deliberately telling impure stories (M)
Deliberately listening to impure stories (M)
Taking pleasure in looking at immodest objects, persons, pictures (M)
Dwelling on immodest objects in thought for some time (D)
Commiting an impure act with another of the same sex or opposite sex (M)
Being unfaithful to one's marriage vow in act (M)
Touching oneself impurely for sake of pleasure (D)
Practicing birth prevention (M)
Reading literature for sex pleasure (M)
Frequenting bad places or persons (M)

Seventh and Tenth Commandments

Being jealous or envious (D)
Stealing something expensive (M)
Stealing something small (V)
Cheating in exams (V), in business (D)
Encouraging others to steal or to accept stolen goods (D)
Damaging another's property (D)
Neglecting one's job seriously (D)

Neglecting to pay a living wage (D)
Neglecting to pay debts (D)

Eighth Commandment

Uncharitable conversation (V)
Telling lies (V) that injured another's good reputation (D)
Talking about the evil of others (D)

Precepts of the Church

Deliberately eating meat on Fridays or days of strict abstinence (M)

Not fasting on days so designated (D) (If in doubt, ask a priest)

Failing to confess at least once a year in case of mortal sin (M)

Failing to receive communion during the Easter Season (First Sunday of Lent to Trinity Sunday) (M)

Receiving communion when knowingly in mortal sin (M)

Not contributing to the support of the Church (D) (If in doubt as to the amount, ask your confessor)

Attempting marriage outside the Church (M)

Attempting to marry a divorced person (M)

Keeping back any serious sin (M)

Having no definite plan of avoiding serious sin in the future (D)

Now say the Act of Contrition (*See* page 80)

How to Confess

SPEAK IN a whisper but distinctly enough to make yourself clear to the priest. If one is hard of hearing, one should seek out a confessional equipped with a hearing aid or go to the priest in the rectory or sacristy of the church.

Usually regular hours for confession are scheduled and listed on the church bulletin. If scheduled hours for confession are not convenient because of work, call the priest at the rectory and he will arrange for a special time.

If the confessional is equipped with lights, it is easy enough to tell when a priest is present and when the penitent's compartment is occupied or empty. As a general rule, when the middle light is on, a priest is present and free. If his light is off and that of the penitent's compartment is on, it indicates that the priest is hearing a confession. If you are uncertain whether a penitent is in the confessional, just wait a while and if no one comes out, you may enter.

Standing or Sitting in Line

WHEN THERE is a great number waiting to go to confession, penitents often sit or stand in line to take their turn in entering the confessional. Remain at a discreet distance from the confessional; far enough away so that you cannot hear what is being said. To avoid the crowded time, it is best to go about the middle of the confession period. Do not hurry your confession because of a long line outside. The priest will govern that.

On entering the confessional, start: "Bless me, Father, for I have sinned; it is (*state period*) since my last Confession." Then confess sins. After this, close with "For these and all the sins of my past life, especially for sins of (*state a past habit of sin*) I am truly sorry and humbly beg pardon and absolution." Answer the necessary questions the priest asks. Feel free to ask the priest any important questions. He will be sympathetic. When the priest asks you to recite the act of contrition, do so in an undertone to assure him you are saying it, but not so loud that those in the church can hear you. If you have forgotten a sin, make note of it and tell it in your next confession.

Saying Penance

IF POSSIBLE, say it immediately after confession, but a penance can be said any time, anywhere.

When to Go to Confession

THE PRECEPT of the Church states that one must go to confession at least once a year. One should go as soon as possible if some serious sin is on his conscience. People who receive communion frequently go to confession at least once every two weeks to be sure that they are in the state of grace, and to keep themselves alert to their sins.

Frequent confession is recommended not only for forgiveness of sin but to prevent it. Through the sacrament of penance, in addition to forgiveness, one receives a twofold help: divine, through special grace; human, through the wise counselling of a confessor.

IT IS POSSIBLE to assist at Mass, even to fulfill one's obligation on Sundays and holydays, without receiving holy communion. While holy communion is the primary fruit of the Holy Sacrifice of the Mass, there are other graces which one can receive by assisting at Mass. However, receiving holy communion at Mass makes assistance at Mass complete and as nearly perfect as it can be. One can have some appreciation of the spiritual value of holy communion by receiving after witnessing the consecration, which is the memorial of Christ's death on Calvary, the price that was paid to make communion possible. The Savior Himself assured us that it was the surest pledge of life everlasting, "He that eateth my flesh and drinketh my blood abideth in me and I in him. And I will raise him up on the last day."

This close and personal union with God here on earth is something we can understand only through divine authority. We would never appreciate it through sentiment or emotions.

Holy communion does not give divine life, that is, sanctifying grace to a soul in mortal sin, any more than food can give life to a dead man. As food restores a sick and weak body to health, so holy communion not only preserves the soul from spiritual death, the downward drag of disordered passions, but by increase of grace will draw the soul closer and closer to God until, like a rocket shot beyond the pull of gravity, the soul free from the pull of concupiscence will become theocentric instead of geocentric.

One is obliged to receive during the Easter Season, which in America extends from the first Sunday of Lent to Trinity Sunday. This is called the Easter Duty and can be fulfilled in any church. One hesitates to speak of holy communion as an obligation. But the Church must direct the faithful to the minimum necessary for the salvation of one's soul.

One should receive as often as the appreciation of it, especially by assisting at Mass, prompts him to do so. At the consecration we have the opportunity of offering to God as the expression of our love the perfect gift of infinite value, to adore Him, serve Him that we may be happy with Him here and perfectly so with Him hereafter. In holy communion He gives His very essence to us, primarily to achieve that goal.

How to receive is given on page 154.

Communion Calls in the Home

AGED AND infirm who cannot attend church regularly should notify the priest and he will bring holy communion to the house. In case of serious illness, the rectory should be notified at any hour of the day or night, and the priest will determine whether the person should receive the last rites. While waiting for the priest to arrive, persons in attendance should help the sick to recite the act of contrition.

Although the following items are not essential and the lack of them should never delay one in calling a priest, they are, where possible, standard equipment in the room of a Catholic who is ill. On a table near the sick bed, covered with a white clean cloth, should be placed a crucifix, two lighted, blessed candles, holy water, a glass of water and spoon, and a clean napkin. If possible,

someone should meet the priest at the door
with a lighted candle in hand and lead him
to the sick person. All present should kneel
out of respect to the Blessed Sacrament
which the priest is carrying. While the priest
hears the patient's confession, all should
leave the room. Quiet should prevail in the
house.

Hospital Cases

THE USUAL practice for a person planning to
enter a hospital is to receive the sacraments of Penance and Holy Eucharist before
entering the hospital. The attending priest
will decide whether a person should receive
the sacrament of extreme unction. If an
emergency case is taken to the hospital in
serious condition, the parish priest should
be notified. Many hospitals, however, have
a resident priest who will take care of emergency cases. Don't delay calling the priest
because the patient "may get upset." In the
event of sudden death, notify the rectory at
once, even if the person may have expired
some time before being discovered.

CONFIRMATION is one of the seven sacraments instituted by Jesus Christ by which
we receive a special grace to make us, as the
name implies, firm and courageous in the
practice of our faith. Converts have need
of this special grace over and above that of
the average Catholic. Becoming a Catholic
usually implies breaking with former ties,
relatives, friends and convictions. In some
cases the step means nothing short of hero-
ism. To live the life of a Catholic in a non-
Catholic environment requires special grace.
Hence converts should receive the sacrament
of confirmation at the first opportunity after
their reception into the Church. In many
dioceses there is a confirmation service held
especially for adults, primarily converts to
the faith. This is announced from the pulpit
at the Sunday Masses. The priest who in-

structed the converts usually notifies them of the time and the church for confirmation for converts.

In confirmation one takes a saint's name other than the one used in baptism.

A sponsor is required for the sacrament of confirmation. Usually one is supplied from the parish, one for the men and one for the women.

It is necessary that the candidate be in the state of grace to receive the graces conferred by confirmation. It is well that one receive the sacrament of penance before being confirmed. It is not necessary to receive holy communion.

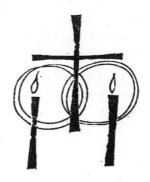

THE PROPER way for two Catholics to marry is with a Nuptial Mass. The bride's pastor has first jurisdiction over the place of the wedding. If the wedding is planned in a church other than that of the bride's parish, permission must be obtained from the bride's pastor. Before setting the date for the wedding, consult the calendar to make sure it will not conflict with a day of fast and abstinence to avoid embarrassing guests at any social function where food is to be served.

The term 'banns of matrimony' means the announcement of an intention to marry. To safeguard the sacrament of matrimony, the Church requires that the intention of two Catholics to marry be announced three successive times at the principal Mass on Sundays or holydays in the respective churches of the couple. This is done to make sure that

69

the engaged couple are free to marry and
that no one knows of any impediment to the
marriage.

In the case of a mixed marriage, where
one party is non-Catholic, usually at least
six instructions are required for the non-
Catholic so he will realize the nature and
purpose of a valid marriage. Hence at least
six weeks should be allowed for arrange-
ments of the marriage with the pastor of the
non-Catholic person. There are no banns
announced in the case of a mixed marriage.

All Catholics must be married in the presence of a priest for the marriage to be valid.
No second religious ceremony can be held, as
it is contrary to the first commandment of
God. Catholics are not allowed to attend a
wedding ceremony of a Catholic marrying
contrary to the laws of the Church, nor are
they allowed to send presents or attend
showers or perform any act that could be
implied as approval of the wedding.

EXTREME UNCTION is administered to a person when he is seriously ill and in danger of death. When a person is seriously ill, the parish priest should be notified as quickly and as eagerly as the doctor. If the person is conscious, the priest will bring not only the holy oil of the infirm with which the person is to be anointed, but also a consecrated particle to give the person viaticum. Holy communion given to a person in danger of death has an added grace and is called viaticum. One receives the priest in the same manner as described under "Communion to the Sick." While waiting for the priest, bystanders should help the sick person to recite the act of contrition.

During the anointing, bystanders kneel and pray for the salvation of the sick person. The priest, after hearing the confession of the sick, and giving him viaticum, will anoint the five senses, saying, "By this holy anointing and His most loving mercy may the Lord pardon you whatever sins you have committed through the sense of hearing." The same is repeated for each of the five senses. After the anointing, the priest gives the apostolic blessing, to which is attached a plenary indulgence if the sick person is in proper disposition. (*See* Indulgences, p. 148.)

If a person should be found unconscious or even dead, notify the priest immediately.

The last rites administered to a person who is still conscious includes confession, communion, extreme unction and the last or apostolic blessing.

Personal and Official Prayer

AS NON-CATHOLICS, converts had an excellent element in their prayers. Stress was placed upon the personal, intimate presence of God, since their prayer, for the most part, was of individual construction, often even spontaneous. It was an intimate conversation with God. While the manner of praying was excellent, the matter might not have been. The common mistake many people make in prayer is to make God's will their will instead of praying to make their way God's way.

In the Catholic Church new converts are frightened at the fact that many prayers are formalized by somebody else and are to be memorized by the convert. Not only that, many prayers in the Church are said in common. All of which leaves the convert rather cold. To make matters worse, common prayers are at times said so fast that one unfamiliar with them can't understand a word.

But in spite of these apparent hindrances to personal prayers, once a new convert has become seasoned in the way of Catholic prayers, we hear such compliments as this— "Isn't that a beautiful prayer!" "I don't want to miss the rosary service." Converts discover that what they have tried to say all

74

along to express their inner appreciation of God and His relationship toward them, has been phrased so much more beautifully by somebody else better versed than they. More important still, the prayer, since it is officially approved by the Church, is absolutely correct and acceptable in the eyes of God. One can put his whole heart, his whole mind, his whole soul into these prayers knowing they express the will of God for him.

Praying in Common

THE FACT that prayers are said in common can even increase their devotional effect. The writer happened to step into church one time during a Holy Hour service. In the pew was a peasant from some Eastern country. He was reciting prayers in common with others—but so devoutly, so distinctly, every word so dedicated, that I can still hear and see him long after it happened. The fact that he was reading prayers composed by another, said in common, only seemed to add to his personal expression of them and his devotion through them.

Converts are still free to say their own prayers in their own way if they prefer. They need not become slaves to any regimentation in prayers or devotions. No prayer is of obligation in the Catholic Church except the assistance at Mass on Sundays and holydays. When they do adopt the prayers of the Church, the benefit and graces acquired by saying prayers will be in direct proportion to the attention and personal application they put into such prayers.

In private prayer, each person has his own personal touch in talking with God—that's what prayer is. It is your means of communing with God in thought and uniting with His will in the affections of your heart. Some pray better with the help of a prayer book; some prefer to read the Scriptures and think on the message of Christ; some prefer to close their eyes and picture Christ in His earthly life; some try to contemplate themselves as part of His life. Again, some prefer to kneel when they pray; others can pray better sitting down. As St. Theresa put it, pray in whatever manner you can pray best. Prayer is like a visit with a friend, near and dear, a conversation with understanding and love.

When to Pray

ABOVE ALL, pray each day and, if possible, at a regular time. St. Paul says, "Pray always." He did not mean that we should be formally engaged in prayer. But all we do, say, and think can be dedicated to the glory of God and the salvation of our souls. This is done by frequently asking the question, "Why am I doing this? What has this to do with Eternal Life?" By *wanting* to do all for the honor and glory of God and the salvation of souls, our whole day becomes a prayer. This is what is meant by "making a general intention."

Why Pray?

PRAYER should have a frequent part in our daily routine to keep us peaceful and happy. The deepest drive in man is a purpose for living. Prayer is the orienting of this life with the next through God's revelation. Prayer means right thinking by looking at God, the author of all Truth, and the attachment of the heart to God as the author of all goodness. Hence, prayer is simply defined as the turning of the mind and heart to God. We look at God, not to analyze Him, not to criticize, find fault. We look at God with admiration, adoration; the perfect One as He revealed Himself, the all-loving, the all-powerful, the all-merciful, the all-knowing Father. The highest motive, the most perfect prayer is to look at God with adoration—that we may become like Him, we, who are made to His image and likeness. In being like Him we will be our true selves. We become like unto the One we adore. The object of adoration is unity between us and God— unity, not by making God to our own image and likeness, but by raising ourselves up to His way, His truth, His life.

We may have difficulties in reconciling things as they are on earth with the Nature and Will of God in Heaven. But if we are humble enough to admit that, while we don't know the answer, that does not mean there is none, then we can pray with our whole mind, heart and soul. "A thousand difficulties need not create one doubt," said Cardinal Newman, a great convert to the Catholic Church.

Following are some suggested prayers. Others may be added according to your choosing.

PRAYERS A CATHOLIC SHOULD MEMORIZE

The Sign of the Cross

IN THE name of the Father, and of the Son, and of the Holy Ghost. Amen.

The Lord's Prayer

OUR FATHER, who art in heaven, hallowed be
Thy name; Thy kingdom come; Thy will be
done on earth as it is in heaven. Give us this
day our daily bread and forgive us our tres-
passes as we forgive those who trespass
against us and lead us not into temptation,
but deliver us from evil. Amen.

The Hail Mary

HAIL, MARY, full of grace! The Lord is with
thee, blessed art thou amongst women, and
blessed is the fruit of thy womb, Jesus. Holy
Mary, Mother of God, pray for us sinners
now and at the hour of our death. Amen.

The Short Doxology

GLORY BE to the Father, and to the Son, and
to the Holy Ghost, as it was in the beginning,
is now, and ever shall be, world without end.
Amen.

The Apostles' Creed

I BELIEVE in God, the Father Almighty, Creator of heaven and earth; and in Jesus
Christ, His only Son, our Lord; who was
conceived by the Holy Ghost, born of the
Virgin Mary, suffered under Pontius Pilate,
was crucified; died and was buried. He

descended into hell; the third day He rose again from the dead; He ascended into heaven, sitteth at the right hand of God, the Father Almighty; from thence He shall come to judge the living and the dead. I believe in the Holy Ghost, the Holy Catholic Church, the communion of Saints, the forgiveness of sins, the resurrection of the body, and life everlasting. Amen.

An Act of Contrition

O MY GOD! I am heartily sorry for having offended Thee, and I detest all my sins, because I dread the loss of heaven and the pains of hell, but most of all because they offend Thee, my God, Who art all-good and deserving of all my love. I firmly resolve, with the help of Thy grace, to confess my sins, to do penance, and to amend my life.

An Act of Contrition (another version)

O MY GOD, I am heartily sorry for having offended You, and I detest all my sins, because of Your just punishments, but most of all because they offend You, my God, who are all-good and deserving of all my love. I firmly resolve, with the help of Your grace, to sin no more and to avoid the near occasions of sin.

An Act of Thanksgiving

O MY GOD! I give You thanks from the bottom of my heart for the mercies and blessings which You have bestowed upon me; above all because You have loved me from all eternity, and have sent Your Divine Son, Our Lord Jesus Christ, to redeem me with His Precious Blood.

An Act of Faith

O MY GOD! I firmly believe that You are one God in three Divine Persons, Father, Son and Holy Ghost; I believe that Your Divine Son became man, and died for our sins, and that He will come to judge the living and the dead. I believe these and all the truths which the Holy Catholic Church teaches, because You have revealed them, who can neither deceive nor be deceived.

An Act of Hope

O MY GOD! Relying on Your infinite goodness and promises, I hope to obtain pardon of my sins, the help of Your grace, and life everlasting, through the merits of Jesus Christ, my Lord and Redeemer.

An Act of Charity

O MY GOD! I love You above all things, with my whole heart and soul, because You are all-good and worthy of all my love. I love my neighbor as myself for the love of You. I forgive all who have injured me and ask pardon of all whom I have injured.

The Morning Offering

O MY GOD, I offer You all my thoughts, words, actions, and sufferings, and I beseech You to give me Your grace that I may not offend You this day. O Sacred Heart of Jesus! I implore that I may ever love You more and more.

The Blessing before Meals

BLESS US, O Lord, and these Your gifts, which we are about to receive from Your bounty, through Christ our Lord. Amen.

Grace after Meals

WE GIVE You thanks for all Your benefits, O Almighty God, who live and reign forever; and may the souls of the faithful departed, through the mercy of God, rest in peace. Amen.

The Angelus

The Angel of the Lord declared unto Mary.
And she conceived by the Holy Spirit. Hail
  Mary, etc.
Behold the handmaid of the Lord,
Be it done unto me according to Your Word.
  Hail Mary, etc.
And the Word was made Flesh,
And dwelt among us. Hail Mary, etc.
Pray for us, O holy Mother of God.
That we may be made worthy of the promises
  of Christ.

Let us pray.

Pour forth, we beg of You, O Lord, Your
grace into our hearts, that we to whom
the Incarnation of Christ Your Son, was
made known by the message of an angel,
may, by His passion and cross, be brought
to the glory of His resurrection, through the
same Christ our Lord. Amen.

Prayer before a Crucifix

Look down upon me, good and gentle Jesus,
while before Your face I humbly kneel, and
with burning soul pray and beseech You, to
fix deep in my heart lively sentiments of
faith, hope, and charity, true contrition for
my sins and a firm purpose of amendment,
while I contemplate with great love and

tender pity, Your five most precious wounds, pondering over them within me, while I call to mind the words which David the prophet spoke of You, my Jesus, "They have pierced my hands and feet; they have numbered all my bones."

Hail, Holy Queen

Hail, Holy Queen! Mother of mercy! Our life, our sweetness and our hope. To thee do we cry, poor banished children of Eve. To thee do we send up our sighs, mourning and weeping, in this valley of tears. Turn, then, most gracious Advocate, thine eyes of mercy toward us and after this our exile show unto us the blessed fruit of thy womb, Jesus. O clement, O loving, O sweet Virgin Mary!

Suggested Morning Prayers

1. Morning Offering
2. Acts of Faith, Hope, Charity
3. The Lord's Prayer

Suggested Evening Prayers

1. Brief examination of conscience—especially on any particular habit of sin.
2. Act of Contrition
3. Act of Thanksgiving
4. The Lord's Prayer

V
DEVOTIONS

DEVOTIONS are specialized prayers approved and encouraged by the Church because of the goodness and virtue they create in souls. They are set prayers arranged for a certain purpose, such as devotions to the Sacred Heart, to stress the love of God for man; devotions to the Blessed Sacrament, to encourage more frequent communion, devotions to the Mother of Christ, such as the novena in honor of the miraculous medal to honor Mary in her Immaculate Conception to cultivate purity in us; rosary devotions to encourage meditation on the great events in the life of our Lord.

There is no obligation to practice any particular devotion. One should cultivate that devotion which he finds most helpful in leading the life of a practical Catholic. One should observe devotions in as much as they bring us closer to Christ and His teaching. The saints are the personification of God's will in human nature like our own. By honoring the virtues of the saints through special devotions, we grow in holiness and approach nearer to God.

Following are some of the more important devotions, a brief description, their purpose and how to observe them.

Devotions to the Blessed Sacrament

ALL DEVOTIONS to the Blessed Sacrament, be it a Holy Hour, Forty Hours, or devotions in Holy Week, are designed to help us appreciate what we are believing—the presence of the Living Christ, under the appearance of bread; and realizing this, we may be desirous of greater union with Christ as God through frequent holy communion.

Benediction

BENEDICTION is a short, impressive and beautiful service. The priest, wearing a cope, opens the tabernacle and takes out a large white host encased in a golden vessel with a glass window (a luro) and inserts it in a gold stand called a monstrance (to show forth). He places this monstrance on a platform and, descending to the foot of the altar, incenses the Blessed Sacrament. Meanwhile, the congregation usually sings the following two hymns to be found on cards or in prayer books, "O Salutaris" and "Tantum ergo Sacramentum."

O Salutaris Hostia

> O Salutaris Hostia
> Quae coeli pandis ostium,

Bella premunt hostilia,
Da robur, fer auxilium.

Uni trinoque Domino
Sit sempiterna Gloria :
Qui vitam sine termino
Nobis donet in patria.

Amen.

O Salutaris Hostia
(*English Translation*)

O Saving Victim, opening wide
The gate of heaven to man below ;
Our foes press on from every side ;
Your aid supply, Your strength bestow.

To Your great Name be endless praise,
Immortal Godhead, One in Three ;
O grant us endless length of days
In our true native land with You.

Amen.

Tantum Ergo

Tantum ergo Sacramentum
Veneremur cernui
Et antiquum documentum
Novo cedat ritui,
Praestet fides supplementum
Sensuum defectui.

Genitori, Genitoque
Laus et jubilatio,
Salus, honor, virtus quoque,
Sit et benedictio,
Procedenti ab utroque,
Compar sit laudatio.
                    Amen.

Tantum Ergo
(*English Translation*)

Down in adoration falling,
Lo, the Sacred Host we hail;
Lo o'er ancient forms departing,
Newer rites of grace prevail;
Faith for all defects supplying,
Where the feeble senses fail.

To the everlasting Father,
And the Son who reigns on high,
With the Holy Ghost proceeding
Forth from each eternally,
Be salvation, honor, blessing,
Might and endless majesty!
                    Amen.

Priest: Panem de coelo praestitisti eis.
          You have given them bread from
          heaven.
People: Omne delectamentum in se ha-
          bentem.
          Containing in itself all sweetness.

At the conclusion of these hymns the priest rises and sings the following prayer in Latin:

O God, who under this wonderful sacrament has left us
a memorial of Your passion; grant us, we beseech You,
so to venerate the sacred mystery of your Body and Blood that
we may ever feel within ourselves the fruit of Your redemption,
who live and reign forever and ever. Amen.

He kneels and receives a special veil over his shoulders. He then ascends the altar and taking the monstrance, holds it with his hands covered by the veil to impress the congregation that the blessing is from God, not the priest, and turning to the people, he makes a large sign of the cross with the monstrance. This is Benediction—the blessing of Christ. Descending the steps, the priest leads the people in the recitation of the Divine Praises:

Blessed be God.
Blessed be His holy name.
Blessed be Jesus Christ, true God and true Man.

Blessed be the name of Jesus.

Blessed be His most Sacred Heart.

Blessed be Jesus in the most holy
sacrament of the altar.

Blessed be the great Mother of God,
Mary most holy.

Blessed be her holy and Immaculate
Conception.

Blessed be the name of Mary, Virgin
and Mother.

Blessed be St. Joseph, her most chaste
spouse.

Blessed be God in His angels and in His
saints.

May the Heart of Jesus in the Most
Blessed Sacrament be praised, adored, and
loved with grateful affection at every moment, in all the tabernacles of the world,
even to the end of time. Amen.

A closing hymn is sung while the priest
places the Blessed Sacrament in the tabernacle.

A Holy Hour

THE LARGE consecrated host is placed in a
monstrance (a stand usually of gold) which
in turn is placed on the altar for public
adoration, amid such sacramentals as candles

and flowers. The hour opens with incensing of the Blessed Sacrament and singing of a hymn. For an hour the congregation is led in meditation by a priest who reads appropriate prayers, gives a sermon. Hymns are sung. The hour ends with Benediction. (*See* Benediction)

The Blessed Sacrament may be placed on the altar and allowed to remain there for the entire day. This is termed, "Exposition of the Blessed Sacrament." The faithful come and adore privately, making a personal visit. The exposition ends with Benediction.

Forty-Hours Devotion

ONCE A YEAR in each parish church a forty-hour devotion in honor of the Blessed Sacrament is celebrated. The devotion opens, usually on Sunday morning, in a solemn manner with a sung Mass and procession. It continues for three days, totaling roughly 40 hours of public adoration to the Blessed Sacrament. The devotion closes in a solemn manner. During this time the faithful receive the sacrament of penance and holy communion. Special graces (*See* Indulgences) are gained by anyone sharing in this devotion.

First Friday Devotion

THE FIRST FRIDAY (of every month) devotion to the Sacred Heart gained momentum through a private revelation to St. Margaret Mary Alacoque, a saintly French nun. Our Lord is said to have appeared to her, showing her His Sacred Heart encircled with a crown of thorns and requested that devotion be given to His Sacred Heart. Thus began devotion to the Sacred Heart on the First Friday of each month. One of the main manifestations of this devotion is the reception of Holy Communion. Out of this grew the devotion known as the Nine First Fridays because of the special graces and blessings promised to those who honored the Sacred Heart this day.

The Sign of the Cross

PRACTICALLY every prayer, private or in common, all devotions, services and blessings begin and end with the Sign of the Cross. The words, together with the formation of the cross, is the profession of our belief in one God and three Divine Persons and in our salvation through the sacrifice of the cross.

Stations of the Cross

THE STATIONS of the Cross, also called the Way of the Cross, is a devotion in honor of the passion and death of our Savior from the judgment of Pilate to the sepulchre. In early days the Way of the Cross was made at the actual scene of our Lord's passion in Jerusalem. Today the Church offers a miniature pilgrimage in one's own church. The Stations are marked by fourteen crosses, usually seven on each side of the church. To aid in meditation, pictures or representations of the various events are placed beneath each cross.

During the Lenten Season, devotions of the Stations of the Cross are held publicly in the church, usually on Fridays. The priest reads the meditations, moving from station to station while the faithful remain in the pews and meditate.

Stations of the Cross can be said privately at any time. For beginners, especially, the use of a prayer book entitled, "Stations of the Cross," is suggested. It will give specific directions how to say the Stations and thoughts for meditation. Two essentials of the devotions are that one meditate on the sufferings of our Savior and move from station to station.

Begin by kneeling at the altar rail for a moment and form the intention of applying the graces attached to this devotion either to the salvation of your own soul or the suffering souls in purgatory. Genuflect before each station, meditate for a while and pass on to the next station. You may kneel at the end of each little meditation and recite the Our Father, Hail Mary and Glory Be for the intention of the Holy Father.

Those who for some reason are unable to make the Stations of the Cross in the place where the crosses have been erected, may do so at home by using a crucifix especially blessed for this purpose.

Rosary

REPETITION of prayer is an ancient custom. It is natural to repeat sayings for emphasis, as one would repeat, "I love you." Various types of "counters" have been used both by pagans and the early Christians, but the one used by Catholics today is called the rosary. The word rosary comes from the Latin word, *rosarium*, which originally meant a garland of roses generally used by the pagans to bestow honor on men and gods, but later came to mean a garland-shaped article.

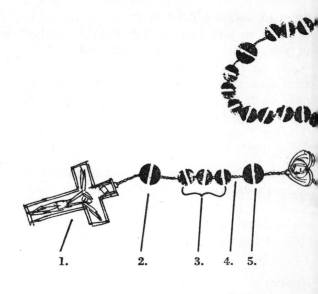

1. Make the Sign of the Cross and say the "Apostles Creed."

2. Say the "Our Father."

3. Say three "Hail Marys."

4. Say the "Glory be to the Father."

5. Announce the First Mystery; then, say the "Our Father."

6. Say ten "Hail Marys."

7. Say the "Glory be to the Father."

8. Announce the Second Mystery; then, say the "Our Father." Repeat 6 and 7.

The rosary may be called a garland of prayers said for a certain purpose. That purpose today is a simple form of meditation on the mysteries of the life of Christ and His Blessed Mother. These mysteries or events are grouped into three sets of five each as listed herein. The diagram illustrates the arrangement of prayers to be said while meditating on a certain mystery. The prayers aid in the meditation as background music is often used during a recitation.

The month of October has been set aside by the Church for special devotion to the rosary. In many churches during the month of October the rosary is recited in public. Most Catholics say the rosary (five mysteries) daily. Certain days are suggested for certain of the mysteries, but there is no obligation in this choice. On Bead No. 5, you are directed in the diagram of the rosary to "announce the first mystery." This means to form your intention on which set of the five mysteries you plan to direct your meditation and then, while meditating on the first mystery of the group, proceed to say the prayers as directed in the diagram.

The method of praying the Rosary is shown by the numbered illustration, pages 96-97.

JOYFUL MYSTERIES
(Monday and Thursday; Advent and Christmas — daily)

1st Mystery — The Annunciation
2nd Mystery — The Visitation
3rd Mystery — The Nativity
4th Mystery — The Presentation
5th Mystery — Finding of the Child in the Temple

SORROWFUL MYSTERIES
(Tuesday and Friday; Lent — daily)

1st Mystery — Agony in the Garden
2nd Mystery — The Scourging
3rd Mystery — Crowning with Thorns
4th Mystery — Carrying the Cross
5th Mystery — Crucifixion

GLORIOUS MYSTERIES
(Wednesdays and Saturdays; Easter Season — daily)

1st Mystery — The Resurrection
2nd Mystery — The Ascension
3rd Mystery — Descent of Holy Ghost on Apostles
4th Mystery — Assumption of Blessed Virgin Mary
5th Mystery — Crowning of Blessed Virgin Mary as Queen of Heaven

On Sundays we meditate on those mysteries which are in the spirit of the liturgical season, for example, Advent, Christmas, Easter, etc.

Devotions to the Sacred Heart

THE CATHOLIC CHURCH considers devotion to the Sacred Heart of Jesus an excellent form of worship. She recommends it to her faithful and grants spiritual favors to those who practice the devotion. The Heart of Jesus is a natural symbol of the infinite charity of the Savior and symbolizes the love of God for men. Societies have been formed among the laity with the special purpose of offering united worship to the Sacred Heart. Among these the best known is the League of the Sacred Heart. Devotion to the Sacred Heart may be private or public. The month of June is especially dedicated by the Church to devotions to the Sacred Heart. Some churches conduct special devotions to the Sacred Heart during the month of June. Standard prayer books contain prayers dedicated to the Sacred Heart.

One of the greatest devotions to the Sacred Heart is that known as the Devotion of the First Fridays of the month. The faithful are urged to receive Holy Communion on the first Friday of each month for nine months in succession, by which they may gain a plenary indulgence. In many churches the Blessed Sacrament is exposed on the altar throughout the day and in the evening special services are conducted in honor of the Eucharistic Lord and especially of His Sacred Heart.

Another growing aspect of this devotion is the "enthronement of the Sacred Heart of Jesus" in the home. A statue or picture of the Sacred Heart is placed in a prominent place in the home to acknowledge the reign of Jesus over the family. The statue or picture is blessed by the priest and the entire family recites an act of consecration to the Sacred Heart, asking Jesus to bless them and grant them the gift of love in their family relationships since all the members love Him.

Novenas

THE WORD novena comes from the Latin word *novem* meaning nine. Hence, a novena of prayers means nine days of prayer. It may be nine consecutive days or a particular day of the week for nine consecutive weeks. A novena is usually made in church publicly, although it can be made privately, either in church or at home. The purpose of the novena prayers is usually to ask for some spiritual blessing or a material blessing insofar as it contributes to the salvation of our souls.

A number of novenas are held in preparation for a particular feast day, and the prayers are directed toward that purpose; for example, Novena to the Holy Spirit before the feast of Pentecost; Novena in honor of the Sacred Heart of Jesus; in honor of the Immaculate Conception; in honor of a saint before his or her feast day.

Novena services generally consist of a sermon, the novena prayers, benediction of the Blessed Sacrament and sometimes veneration of a relic.

Veneration of the Saints

ONE of the official marks of sanctity usually required by the Church is two authenticated, first-class miracles. This is proof that a certain person has found favor with God, is His special elect. Because of this, public prayers are permitted which take the form of veneration, not adoration. God alone is adored by Catholics. To pray to saints means to admire them and become like them and, therefore, to become nearer in our likeness to the image of God.

Communion of Saints

THE COMMUNION of Saints is the term used to indicate that the saints, because of their union with us in the mystical body of Christ, can communicate with us and help us both in this life and the next. The term Communion of Saints also means that all baptized Christians are united in the one world-wide family of God. The term *saint* as used here and in the Apostles' Creed has the same meaning as in the New Testament, that is, a baptized Christian.

SACRAMENTALS are audio-visual aids, approved and blessed by the Church as a means of obtaining grace. They include words, actions, objects that, through the senses, direct man's mind and heart to the invisible spiritual good which is God; and thus they become a means of grace. They should be used only for the purpose of inspiring deeper understanding and devotion to the faith. Converts may be slow to use these external signs, since their purpose and use are often misrepresented and misunderstood by the non-Catholic mind. It is not the proper use but the abuse of sacramentals that has created an attitude of aversion toward sacramentals among non-Catholics. Two extremes are to be avoided in the use of all sacramentals.

106

1. Do not despise them as superstitious.

2. Do not consider them as infallible charms against temporal calamities or as endowed with miraculous powers. Only so far as their use leads one nearer to God can one expect to receive grace and divine protection through them.

Space allows the mention of only some of the more important and most commonly used sacramentals:

Sign of the Cross

THE SACRAMENTAL that stands first in dignity and the one most commonly used both in public and private worship is the sign of the cross. It is both a symbol of the way of our redemption and our profession of belief in the Holy Trinity. It summarizes God's relationship toward us. He is the Creator, the Savior and the Sanctifier. Catholics begin and end all important prayer with the sign of the cross.

Candles

GOD MANIFESTED His presence by means of light in the Old Testament. Christ referred to Himself as the Light of the World. Light in the form of candles was probably first

used by Christians to light up the darkness
of the catacombs and for services before
dawn. Their use was soon associated with
sacred worship.

Though not necessary to the validity of a
sacrament, candles are now used by the
Church to enhance the beauty of all sacraments except that of penance. Custom has
decreed that a definite number of candles be
used for different occasions. For example:
at a Pontifical Mass 7 candles are used; at
a Solemn Mass, 6 candles; at a Pontifical
Low Mass or a Sung Mass, 4 candles are
sufficient; at all low Masses, 2 candles.

Candles are also used at many devotional
services, as votive candles before a shrine
and during sick calls made to the home by
a priest. For this latter purpose, Catholics
should keep blessed candles in their homes.
(*See* Sick Calls)

Votive candles are the ones in which converts are usually more directly interested.
The use of these candles, which are not
blessed, is not a sacramental and is entirely
optional on the part of the Catholic. Placed
before a shrine or a statue, their flickering
light gives beauty and serenity to the sometimes gloomy interior of the church. Origi-

nally, they were lit by the faithful to signify the fulfillment of a vow; hence the term 'votive' from the Latin *votum,* meaning vow. Today it has become more of a symbolic act whereby the Catholic goes to the shrine of his favorite saint, lights a candle, kneels and prays that he may keep with him during the day the particular virtue, such as humility, for which that saint is noted.

A *canon candle* is liturgically correct, although most of the churches do not use it today. It is a special candle lit at the Sanctus, that is, the beginning of the Canon of the Mass, and allowed to burn until after the communion of the Mass. This is to let the faithful know when the solemn part of the Mass begins and ends.

The *sanctuary lamp,* usually consisting of a hanging glass vessel encased in a beautiful and especially designed frame, burns day and night before an altar where the Blessed Sacrament is kept. It is the sure sign of the Real Presence. Sometimes three or even seven lamps are used instead of one. The color of the glass may be white, transparent or red. In some churches, the sanctuary light is a standing instead of a hanging lamp.

Holy Water

AS WATER is a natural element of cleansing, so its use, when blessed, is a symbol of spiritual purification. Water, when blessed, is called holy water. There are several types of blessing. The ordinary holy water is blessed by the priest with solemn prayers asking God's protection of those who use it. The water may be blessed at any time. It may be used by the individual lay person, especially in making the sign of the cross, primarily when entering the church. It may be used in the home for the same purpose. Holy water fonts for the home may be obtained at the religious goods stand in the parish church or in Church Goods stores.

Holy water is used by the priest for nearly all blessings of persons, places and things.

Easter Water

EASTER WATER is holy water which is blessed only on Holy Saturday with greater solemnity and given to the faithful only at that time.

Baptismal Water

BAPTISMAL WATER is holy water which is blessed on Holy Saturday (this being the liturgical time for receiving converts into the Church) with a solemn blessing, including the use of holy oils. It is used only for the administration of the sacrament of baptism. In case of baptism in emergency regular water may be used.

Asperges

THE ASPERGES is the sprinkling of the congregation with holy water before the celebration of a sung Mass on Sunday. As the celebrant sprinkles the congregation, the choir sings from Psalm 50, "Cleanse me of sin with hyssop, O Lord, that I may be purified; wash me and I shall be whiter than snow." The sprinkling with holy water thus has a symbolic meaning—to cleanse the mind from all evil distractions that might hinder a person in proper assistance at Mass.

Incense

INCENSE IS a granulated aromatic resin obtained from certain trees in the East. When mixed with spices and placed on burning coals, it gives off a white smoke of fragrant odor. Incense symbolizes the prayers of the faithful ascending before the throne of God. Hence, incense is used at Solemn Mass, Benediction and other solemn services. The use of incense in worship not only dates back to the early days of the Old Testament, but to pagan worship as well.

In Catholic worship incense is used by placing it on live coals carried in a vessel in the form of a bowl suspended by chains so that it can be swung to and fro to diffuse the smoke and fragrance. This vessel is called a censer.

Ashes

ASHES, blessed on Ash Wednesday, are remnants of burned palm kept from the preceding Palm Sunday. Solemnly blessed at the altar before the principal Mass, they are placed on the foreheads of Catholics in the form of a cross by the priest with the words: "Remember man that you are dust and unto dust you shall return." This ceremony has ever emphasized the need of penance and humility in our lives.

The new Catholic should find out at what times the ashes are distributed in his parish church or in a church near his business, and be present to receive this sacramental on Ash Wednesday.

Palms

PALM is one of the most solemnly blessed articles of the Church. Given out on Palm

Sunday, these symbols of Christ's earthly triumph should be kept carefully until the following Palm Sunday and then burned or disposed of in a fitting manner. A common custom is to place the blessed palm near a crucifix or holy picture in the home.

Scapular

THE SCAPULAR, originally limited to use by men and women in religious orders, consists of two strips of cloth the width of the shoulders and extending to the ankles, one strip in front, the other over the back of the person. Because of its shape it symbolizes the yoke of Christ.

Today a similar but shorter scapular, extending to the waist is worn by men and women belonging to the secular tertiaries, who wear it under their regular clothing.

For the lay person, the scapular consists of two pieces of cloth about two inches by three inches, joined by a string and worn underneath the clothing. The best known of such scapulars is the brown scapular. The blessings of God are invoked by the Church on the wearers. A medal blessed for this purpose may be substituted for this scapular.

Medals

MEDALS ARE pieces of metal on which pictures of our Lord, our Lady, the saints or events in history are usually die cut. As sacramentals, they are blessed. Chief among these are the scapular medal, the miraculous medal and the St. Christopher medal.

Miraculous Medal

THE MIRACULOUS MEDAL commemorates a vision of our Lady received by Saint Catherine Labouré in the Paris convent of the Sisters of Charity. On one side it bears the image of Mary standing on a globe. Around this picture are the words: "O, Mary, Conceived without Sin, Pray for Us Who Have Recourse to Thee." On the reverse side there is a large M surmounted by a cross and surrounded by twelve stars. Beneath are the hearts of Jesus and Mary; the one crowned with thorns, the other pierced by a sword.

St. Christopher Medal

THE ST. CHRISTOPHER MEDAL is commemorative of an early Christian by that name who, according to legend, once carried Christ, who appeared to him in the form of a child, across a dangerous river. St. Christopher is the patron of travelers, and St. Christopher medals are frequently carried in automobiles and worn on airplane trips.

Scapular Medal

THE SCAPULAR MEDAL is frequently worn in place of the cloth scapular by lay persons. People must be enrolled in the scapular before they can wear the scapular medal. It must be blessed by a priest. The medal usually has a picture of our Lord with His Sacred Heart on one side and on the other, the image of our Lady.

Statues

STATUES, like medals and relics, are sacramentals used in religious devotion to direct one's thoughts to the virtues of the saint whom the statue represents. One prays before a statue not *to* a statue. The presence of statues in church by no means invites idolatry because statues are not idols of things on earth but symbols of the saints in heaven, the especially elect of God To venerate, not adore, a statue, brings one closer to God, whose will the saints personified in human flesh and blood.

Relics

RELICS ARE fragments of the bones of saints or pieces of clothing or any object intimately connected with their persons which have been preserved out of respect for their heroic sacrifice. Often, after public devotions to a saint, there is the veneration of his relic. The faithful approach the communion rail and kiss the relic. There is no obligation to do so, but neither are we to ridicule such devotion, since it is permitted by the Church and, therefore, acceptable to God. To venerate a relic is not idolatry. God alone is worthy of adoration. He is the source of grace and the life of perfection. The saints are His specially beloved, the personification of God's will in human flesh and blood, and the channels of God's grace. By cultivating devotion to saints by venerating their relics, we become more like them in virtue and therefore closer to God.

VII
FASTING
AND
ABSTINENCE

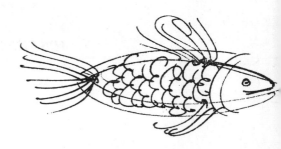

BODILY mortification was practiced by the Orientals even before it was emphasized in Christian revelation. In Christian living, asceticism of any type has primarily a spiritual motive, denying the sense appetites not only all excess indulgence, but even legitimate indulgence to do penance for past sins and prevent future mastery of the body over the spiritual life of the soul. "Do penance or you shall all likewise perish."

Fasting and abstinence are two fruitful ways of fulfilling this divine admonition. The Church, knowing the will of God and the needs of human nature, offers principles to apply this natural and positive divine law of penance to our times and under present working conditions. Fasting means limiting the quantity of food. Abstaining, in the sense

used by the Church, means refraining from eating meat on appointed days.

As working conditions change, the Church has adapted the laws of fasting and abstinence according to human needs. The Church does not intend that penance should be done to the degree of injuring one's health or lessening normal efficiency at work. Both fasting and abstinence are limited to certain days and for good reasons and to persons according to age.

Abstinence

TO DO without certain kinds of food means to abstain. As used by the Church, it means to abstain from meat and its products. Abstinence may be partial or complete.

119

Complete abstinence means no meat at all on appointed days, which include all Fridays, Ash Wednesday, the day before the Feast of the Immaculate Conception and the day preceding Christmas Eve. When meat is forbidden, so are soups and gravy made from meat.

Partial Abstinence. Meat is allowed once a day at the principal meal. The days for this observance are Wednesdays and Saturdays of Ember Week and the day before Pentecost. The Ember days will be announced at Mass of the previous Sunday.

Who are bound by the law of abstinence? Normally, *everyone* over seven years of age.

Fasting

FASTING LIMITS the quantity of food to one full meal a day, either at noon or in the evening, and two partial meals sufficient in quantity to maintain strength. Together they should not equal a full meal. Fasting also limits the use of meat to once a day at the full meal except on days of complete abstinence as stated above.

When To Fast

ALL WEEKDAYS of Lent (Ash Wednesday and Holy Saturday to midnight inclusive), the

Ember days (Wednesdays, Fridays and Saturdays at the beginning of the four seasons of the year), the Vigils of Pentecost and the Immaculate Conception, and December 23. (These days will be announced from the pulpit the previous Sunday.)

Sundays and holydays are never days of fast or abstinence. Public holidays may not be, depending upon the ruling of the bishop in whose diocese you live.

Who Must Fast?

EVERYONE OVER 21 and under 59 years of age are bound to the law of fasting unless excused as explained below. Eating between meals is not permitted. Liquids, including milk (not milk shakes), fruit juices, alcoholic beverages are permitted between meals. Medicines, whether solid or liquid, may be taken at any time.

You may wonder what is the difference between the days of fasting and partial abstinence with reference to eating meat, since both rules allow meat once a day. The difference lies in the persons who come under the rule. On days of partial abstinence, all must abstain from 7 years of age and over. On days of fasting, only persons over 21 and under 59 years of age are bound to abstain.

Eucharistic Fast

THIS IS the fasting required in preparation for the reception of holy communion. It can be summarized in these simple statements:

1. Water is allowed any time.
2. Liquids (anything that can be taken through a straw), except alcoholic beverages, may be taken up to one hour before receiving holy communion.
3. Solid foods and alcoholic beverages up to three hours before holy communion.
4. Medicines, solid or liquid (non-alcoholic), can be taken at any time.

Dispensations

SINCE THE laws of fast and abstinence are Church laws, the Pope, directly or indirectly through the bishops and priests, can relax these laws when certain circumstances make it very difficult for the faithful to keep them; for example, fast days falling on public holidays; places where it is difficult to get seafood; in the armed services where there is little or no choice of menu.

Physical or moral impossibility excuses individuals from the law of fasting; for example, the sick or convalescent; those subject to bad headaches; pregnant or nursing women; people engaged in hard manual labor.

In case of any doubt the person should consult a priest in or outside of the confessional, and let him judge whether the circumstances excuse the person from the law of fast.

For a general dispensation from the law of fast or abstinence, one must consult the pastor who has the power to dispense.

VIII
LENT
AND
HOLY
WEEK

THE CHURCH, in remembrance of the forty
days of fast of Christ in the desert and as
a means of sanctification of the faithful, has
designated the forty days, excluding Sundays, preceding Easter, as a season of penance and a time for special meditation on
the passion and death of the Savior. Penance
takes the form of fasting and abstinence.
(*See* chapter VII for rules and regulations.)
In the liturgy of the Church, the whole tone
is penitential. The color of the vestments is
purple. The joyful notes in the Masses are
omitted, such as the *Gloria,* the *Alleluia,* and
even the organ music. The Epistles, Gospels
and prayers concentrate on the theme of
penance in general and the sorrowful events
in the life of Christ.

On the fourth Sunday of Lent, in the
middle of the season, the liturgy assumes a

note of joy. Rose-colored vestments are worn, a compromise between the penitential purple and the white of Easter. "Rejoice, you who have been in sorrow," says the words of the *Introit*. Rejoice that you have persevered thus far; relax for a day before resuming the journey up the hill of Calvary.

On the fifth Sunday, you will find all images in the Church, especially the Crucifix, veiled in purple and they will remain so until the unveiling on Good Friday. This symbolizes concentration of the liturgy on the passion of our Lord. Hence the sixth Sunday, Palm Sunday, begins Holy Week, which is devoted, in the liturgy, to the final events in our Lord's passion. During this week, the Church has several special services which converts find not only devotional but inspiring. There is a special missal for this week, Holy Week Missal, which is a must if we are to follow and appreciate the liturgical services of this week. The newer Daily Missals also contain the services of Holy Week.

Palm Sunday

HOLY WEEK opens with Palm Sunday, which commemorates the triumphal entry of Christ into Jerusalem. This event occurred in the life of Christ shortly before His crucifixion.

In memory of this act of profession of faith
in Christ by His followers, the Church blesses
palm and distributes it to the faithful who
take part in the procession which precedes
the Mass itself. Only recently the Holy
Father has urged bishops and pastors to
stress this service and give the congregation
a real part in this public profession in the
divinity of their Savior, through whose hu-
manity they were saved on Calvary. The
prayer said by the priest after the procession
encourages the faithful to take home the
palm as a reminder of the loyalty they pledge
Christ on this day of triumph.

Holy Thursday

ON HOLY THURSDAY the Church commemorates the Last Supper and the institution of
holy communion. All the faithful are urged
to participate by receiving holy communion.
For the convenience of the people, Mass is
celebrated morning, noon and night, and
Holy Communion distributed at all hours.
After the final and solemn services, the death
of the Lord is observed; all bells and organ
music cease. The Blessed Sacrament is removed from the main altar, the tabernacle
left open, empty, and the altar stripped of
all the externals reminding one of the real
presence.

After this Mass, the Blessed Sacrament is removed to a special side altar provided with a repository. Here, in the midst of externals, candles, flowers, etc., the faithful take turns keeping prayerful watch until the Blessed Sacrament is removed for the communion service on Good Friday.

Good Friday

ON GOOD FRIDAY no Mass is said. In spirit the faithful are taken back to the first Mass on Calvary. The main liturgical service is the unveiling and the solemn veneration of the cross. The celebrant and assistants solemnly venerate it first by approaching the cross without shoes. Then the faithful come to the communion rail to "kiss the cross." It is sufficient to kiss the feet of the image.

After the solemn veneration of the cross, holy communion is distributed, fittingly enough, since on Good Friday was merited the grace which we receive in holy communion. The particles were consecrated on Holy Thursday since no Mass is celebrated on Good Friday. The services, heretofore referred to as the Mass of the Pre-sanctified, is only a communion service.

Holy Saturday

ON HOLY SATURDAY the Vigil of the Resurrection, the Church in her liturgy attempts to follow the time of day as well as the events that preceded the Resurrection. Services start in the evening, ending in time for Mass at midnight. The significant thing about the services, especially for converts and prospective converts, is that the service centers around baptism, since in the early Church, catechumens were baptized at this service. The entire service proceeds in spirit from darkness to light. It begins with the blessing of the new fire (the church is in complete darkness) and the Easter candle, symbols of Christ's Resurrection, and the chanting of prophecies, originally intended for the instruction of catechumens in preparation for baptism. This is followed by the blessing of baptismal water to be used during the year. At the conclusion of the Vigil services, the Mass of the Resurrection is celebrated.

IX
BLESSINGS

A BLESSING is the rite by which the Church dedicates persons, places and things to a sacred purpose and attaches to them a spiritual value in their proper use. Non-Catholics are capable of receiving them with certain exceptions. A priest can bless any person any time. It is proper to ask for a priest's blessing, especially when he visits the home or a sick person whether at home or in the hospital.

BLESSING OF PERSONS

Apostolic Blessing

THE APOSTOLIC BLESSING is the Pope's blessing. It can be imparted to the dying by a priest under certain circumstances; at the closing of a mission, a retreat, or a novena. A plenary indulgence is attached to this blessing when received under the usual conditions. (*See* Indulgences)

Churching

THIS BEAUTIFUL ceremony, which is the blessing of a woman after childbirth, occurs when the mother is able to go to church. It recalls Mary going to God's temple for her legal purification forty days after her Child's birth.

The ceremony usually takes place after Mass. The mother approaches the priest and asks to be churched. The priest, vested in surplice and stole, comes to the communion rail. A blessed and lighted candle is given to the mother to hold while the priest reads prayers of praise and thanksgiving for the safe delivery of child and mother and petitions God that "she and her offspring may deserve to obtain the joys of eternal happiness." During the prayers the priest offers the mother the end of the stole which she holds and may kiss. This is symbolic of her being led into the Church by him to offer thanks. He sprinkles her with holy water and bestows a blessing upon her.

This ceremony is not obligatory.

Nuptial Blessing

IN THE celebration of a Nuptial Mass, the priest makes two interruptions in order to give the bride the special blessing the Church wishes for her. After saying the Lord's Prayer at Mass, the priest turns to the bride and in part prays "that she may be dear to her husband like Rachel; wise like Rebecca; long-lived and faithful like Sara. May (she and her husband) see their children's children unto the third and fourth generation."

Before blessing the congregation near the end of the Mass, the priest pauses again to pray for the bride: "May the God of Abraham, the God of Isaac and the God of Jacob be with you and may He fulfill His blessing in you, etc."

Blessing of Sick

THERE IS a special blessing for people who are sick. This blessing can be given and should be asked for even when sickness is not grave but prolonged.

Blessing of Throats

ON FEBRUARY 3, Catholics and non-Catholics throng the churches to receive the blessing of St. Blaise, who is the patron saint of those afflicted with throat ailments. The priest prays that the recipient "through the intercession of St. Blaise" be protected from any evil, especially such as may harm the throat.

BLESSING OF PLACES

Blessing of Homes

IT IS customary for families to ask their priest to bless their homes. He invokes God's protection on the house or apartment and all who dwell therein; and, as he recites the beautiful prayers, he sprinkles each room with holy water. Either the father or mother should lead him through the rooms which are to be sprinkled.

Blessing homes during Easter Week with solemnly blessed Easter water is common in certain countries.

BLESSING OF THINGS

Blessing of Articles

SCAPULARS, medals, rosaries, candles, statues, crucifixes, pictures, automobiles, airplanes and practically everything that has a lasting quality of existence may be blessed by a priest. Objects blessed do not lose the blessing by being broken and repaired or by being lent or given away, but only by being sold or totally destroyed.

X
CHRISTIAN SYMBOLS

A RELIGIOUS symbol is a material object representing some spiritual truth. The use of symbols by the Church dates back to the days of the catacombs. In days of persecution, Christians used a sign language which at one and the same time would hide and represent truths which they could not outwardly portray because of ridicule and desecration. Later on the Church used them as a direct and decorative medium of presenting truths, rich in meaning. To this day you will see symbols in the paintings of the Church, stained glass windows, vestments, altars.

Symbols may be objects of nature, animals, plants, initial letters, and objects used, at least formerly, in the ritual of the Church, such as a sea shell as the symbol of Baptism.

Animals as Symbols

The *fish*, a favorite emblem of the early Christians, is a symbol of our Blessed Lord. The Greek word for fish is ichthus, which combines the initial letters of the Greek words for Jesus Christ, Son of God, Savior.

The *dove* is the symbol of the Holy Spirit. At the baptism of Christ, the New Testament tells how the Holy Spirit descended upon Him in the visible sign of a dove.

The *lamb* was an emblem in the Old Testament, where it prefigured Christ, our Savior. In the New Testament, from John the Baptist to John the Evangelist's *Apocalypse*, the Savior is referred to as "The Lamb of God." The lamb is represented sometimes as bearing a cross or a banner on which the cross

139

is inscribed. Sometimes the lamb is pictured lying slain on a book bearing seven seals as described in the *Apocalypse*, the last book of the Bible.

The *pelican*, pictured with beak on its breast feeding its young with its own blood, is a symbol of our Lord who through the shedding of His blood merited the grace which we receive especially in the Holy Eucharist.

The *dragon* represents Satan and sin, and is usually shown as conquered by the power of good, symbolized by St. Michael, the Archangel.

The *serpent*, the emblem of sin, often seen beneath the feet of the Blessed Virgin, in

her role as the Immaculate Conception, symbolizes the Scriptural text of Genesis, "the seed of the woman shall crush his head." When twined around a cross the serpent is emblematic of the brazen serpent raised up by Moses in the desert—prefiguring our Savior.

Symbolic Plants

The *olive branch*, emblem of peace, is shown in the hand of the Archangel Gabriel, in the hands of martyrs symbolizing their peace of soul in heavenly repose.

The *lily*, perhaps the most commonly seen, represents chastity. We see it associated with the Annunciation, St. Joseph, and with saints noted for the virtue of purity, St. Anthony, St. Aloysius.

The *rose*, the emblem of beauty and love, is symbolic of Mary in her title of "Mystical Rose."

Shafts of *wheat* and bunches of *grapes* symbolize the Holy Eucharist.

Letters and Other Objects

The *letters* AΩ, the first and last letters of the Greek alphabet, signify God as the beginning and end of all things. (*See* p. 10.)

A *triangle* with an eye pictured in the center represents the Trinity and in the center the all-seeing eye of God.

The *Circle,* the perfect mathematical figure, without beginning or end, symbolizes God as the Infinite Being in time.

The *monogram* ⊗ superimposed, usually stands for the Greek letters chi and rho, equivalent to Ch and R in English, the first two Greek letters of the word, Christ, which were used instead of the whole word. The

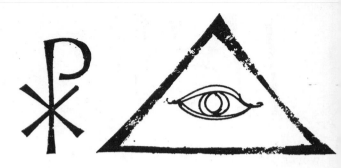

letters IHS most frequently used by the Church is again an abbreviation of the Greek for the name Jesus, the E in Greek being shaped like the English letter H.

INRI on the inscription of a crucifix stands for the phrase, Jesus of Nazareth, King of the Jews, the inscription ordered by Pontius Pilate to be hung on the Cross of Christ. The letters stand for the inscription in Latin, which uses an I in place of J, Iesus Nazarenus Rex Iudaeorum."

The monogram *AM* superimposed stands for Ave Maria, hence the Blessed Mother.

The emblem of *keys crossed*, sometimes with the pope's tiara, is symbolic of the power of the pope to bind and loose, "I will give to you the keys of the Kingdom of Heaven."

I·N·R·I

A *candle* typifies Christ "the light of the world." Sometimes the seven branched candlestick is used to signify the seven sacraments or seven gifts of the Holy Spirit.

Christ, His Blessed Mother and saints are ornamented with a *halo* symbolizing their life of grace and sanctity. Sometimes there is added the symbol of the particular virtue of the saint or position which he graced, as mitre and staff for bishops a crucifix for missionaries; and a crown of thorns for noted ascetics or martyrs.

A *ship* symbolizes the Church, the bark of Peter, often pictured on the stormy sea of life.

The *anchor* is a symbol of hope, being the chief safety in time of danger. It is combined at times with the cross, the emblem of faith, and the heart, emblem of love.

XI
INDULGENCES
RETREATS
STIPENDS

Indulgences

THE WORD indulgence (in + dulcis — sweetness, generousness), when first used by the Church meant to grant grace for doing penance. In popular use today, it has the connotation of lack of penance, something soft, as indulgent parents. The uninformed often attach this latter meaning to the doctrine of indulgences. They think it means getting something for nothing.

To understand rightly the origin and the proper use of indulgences, a few facts must be understood. After sin is forgiven, there remains the punishment due to sin which must be remitted. It is of two kinds; eternal, which God alone can remit; temporal (which lasts only for a while), which we can remit by doing penance, either here or hereafter.

Indulgences offer a possible and fruitful means of discharging our debt of temporal punishment still remaining after our sins are forgiven. Through His passion and death, the Savior merited for us the remission of all punishment due to sin. From the treasure of grace merited by Christ and His saints, especially those who shed their blood for the Faith, the Church offers partial substitutes in the form of indulgences for the punishment the faithful have deserved.

The Church offers a partial substitute for punishment due to sin. The sinner must fulfill certain conditions to prove himself worthy and meritorious of such graces. To gain an indulgence, one must be in a state of grace, and do certain prescribed penance. Confession is required to assure that the person is in the state of grace.

A plenary (full) indulgence removes all punishment due to sin. A partial indulgence removes only part of it. The amount of partial indulgences gained is measured relatively by the penance performed by the early Christians to remove punishment due to their sins. Thus the number 40 days, 5 years, and so forth, means that an amount of punishment is removed corresponding to 40 days, 5 years, and so forth, of doing penance in the literal way in which the Church imposed penance on sinners in the early centuries of Christianity. The notation 5 years after a certain prayer means that if you are in a state of grace and say this prayer, you will gain as much merit as you would have gained by doing a certain penance yourself for 5 years. Only God knows absolutely how much temporal punishment remains to be removed.

Most plenary indulgences can be gained only once during each day. If it can be gained several times the notation, *Toties Quoties* (as often as you fulfill the conditions) is added. Another notation is often expressed by the phrase, "under the usual conditions," which include:

1. Visit to a public chapel or church.

2. Prayer for the intention of the Holy Father, usually by saying one *Our Father, Hail Mary* and *Glory Be.*

3. Confession within eight days before or after performing the penance.

4. Receive holy communion within eight days of performing the indulgenced work.

The indulgences can be applied to oneself or to the suffering souls in purgatory, but to no other living person.

We cannot be certain that we have gained a plenary indulgence in its fullness. To do so, one must be detached completely from all deliberate sin, venial as well as mortal. This is a high requirement. If we do not gain a plenary indulgence, we can still gain a partial indulgence while trying for the plenary indulgence.

Retreats

BECAUSE the pressure of business and busy schedules leave little time to think or pray, special places and times are set aside whereby those who seek rest of mind and peace of soul may withdraw or "retreat" from the world and commune with God by spending a day or weekend in thinking and praying. This is usually done at a retreat house provided by the diocese, one for men and one for women. Retreats are growing in popularity, apparently because people feel the need. Converts are urged to make at least a day of retreat within one year of their reception into the Church. See your parish priest for information. An annual day of recollection or, better still, a week-end retreat is a must as a preventive for spiritual stagnation.

Stipends

THE FINANCIAL support of the pastor, as well as the expense for administration of the parish, come from free-will offerings of the parishioners. One source of such support is the stipend or donation offered the priest for any special personal service, such as marrying a couple, baptizing a baby, and especially offering a Mass for the person's private intention.

All pastors are obliged to offer a Mass expressly for the intention of the parishioners on Sundays and holydays. On other days he can offer a Mass for anyone's personal request. For this it is customary to offer a donation, which varies in amount with the particular diocese. Such donations should not be looked upon as 'payment' for the spiritual favor. When in doubt a convert can always ask some Catholic what the customary stipend is for any personal service, or telephone the rectory and ask the priest.

XII
HOW
TO . . .

Receive Holy Communion

WHEN THE celebrant consumes the consecrated wine (this is usually obvious since you can see him raise the chalice to his lips), approach the altar rail, hands folded in a spirit of reverence. No rushing is necessary. If large numbers are receiving, directions may be given to approach by the center aisle and return by side aisles.

When the priest approaches you, raise your head, open your mouth and extend your tongue to rest on and cover your lower lip. After receiving, return with hands folded and eyes downcast. Loosen the host with the tongue and swallow it. Do not touch it with the finger. Do not worry about the sacred host touching the teeth. Let the thoughts be simple and few, adoration, thanksgiving, acts of love.

Make the Sign of the Cross

WITH THE right hand touching the forehead, say "In the name of the Father," then touching the breast, add "and of the Son," then touching the left shoulder and crossing over and touching the right shoulder, add, "And of the Holy Spirit," and dropping the hand say, "Amen."

154

In reading the Gospel, a triple sign of the cross is made by tracing a small cross with the thumb on the forehead, the lips and the breast. This is to remind us that our intellect must be attentive to the word of God, our lips ready to proclaim it and our heart pure to follow it.

Venerate the Cross (See Holy Week)

Enter a Church

IT IS CUSTOMARY to dip the first two fingers into the holy water and make the sign of the cross as usual. The holy water is a reminder to purify our hearts and minds upon entering before the Real Presence. Before entering the pew, genuflect in acknowledgment of the Real Presence by bending the right knee until it touches the floor, keeping the body erect. We can steady ourselves by resting the left hand or both hands on the left knee. Enter the pew and kneel in prayer. Recollect God's presence in the blessed sacrament and make a brief act of adoration. Then proceed with any devotion one has in mind.

Should one enter while the blessed sacrament is exposed on the altar, make a profound genuflection by kneeling on both knees and bowing the head and upper body.

In leaving the church, one uses the same ritual as entering the church. However, the holy water is meant to be used primarily when entering before the Real Presence.

Men should be neatly attired, even if in working clothes because of a job on Sundays. The attire of women should be modest, and they are expected to have their heads covered. Paper napkins or similar objects are poor excuses for a head covering. Chewing gum is in bad taste in church, as is leaving the church during the sermon to take a smoke.

Standing in the back of the church when there are plenty of seats or insisting on sitting on the end of the bench and forcing others to crawl over you is bad manners. Silence is observed at all times. This precludes whispering the rosary audibly.

When the hands are not clasping a rosary or prayer book, it is customary to fold them in prayer. Folded hands are a sign of recollection and should be especially done when going to communion. Rushing out of church before the celebrant has left the altar is a sure sign of lack of generosity with God.

Register in One's Parish

CALL AT the parish house and ask for the pastor. If he is not available, one of the assistant priests can take care of the matter. Just tell the priest that you have come to register in the parish. Registering in one's parish church is important for the better care of souls, for sick calls and for administration of the parish. Catholics have an obligation to support their parish church financially. Although it is not necessary that they attend their parish church to fulfill the obligation of attending Mass on Sundays, they are urged to do so and to affiliate themselves with parish activities and societies. The parish church should be the family church.

Arrange for a Wedding

CATHOLICS planning to marry should call upon the pastor of the girl six weeks or more before the proposed date for the wedding. If the wedding is to take place at Mass, the pastor of the girl should be notified a couple of months in advance so that a reservation for the hour of the Mass can be arranged. Normally, banns are announced, which usually requires three weeks. Necessary papers, baptismal records of both parties, and letters of freedom to marry must be secured.

In case one of the couple is a non-Catholic, consult the pastor of the Catholic party at least four, preferably more, weeks in advance.

Have a Mass Said for Your Intention

CALL at the rectory and make your request known to anyone who answers the door. If you wish a Mass card, which is the usual thing in case of a death, the priest will arrange one for you. The offering for the Mass varies. Let the priest tell you of the customary offering.

Arrange for Baptism of a Baby

NORMALLY, the hour for baptisms is announced from the pulpit or put into the parish bulletin. If so, just appear at the church at that hour. A priest will be present to take care of you. If no regular hour is announced, telephone the rectory. At least one, preferably two, practical Catholics must be invited as sponsors.

See Baptism, pages 44-47.

XIII
SUPPLEMENTARY
READING

ON THE EVE of reception into the Church, converts invariably feel that their knowledge and understanding of the great truths taught by the Catholic Church is most incomplete. This is nearer the truth, perhaps, than they themselves even realize. Time did not allow them to read all of the pamphlets or books assigned during the course of instructions. Not only for further information and better understanding of the Catholic Faith, but especially for progress in the spiritual life, further reading is a must. The spiritual life, like the physical is something living and must grow to stay alive. Next to the sacraments and prayer, the most fruitful way to grow in holiness is profitable reading.

Following is a suggested list of books selected especially with new converts in mind. Almost all can be obtained in the inexpensive paperback editions. Every convert should have a shelf of these standard books which will become his constant companions in his daily reading and living.

The list is classified under general headings and according to intellectual background to help the convert in making a suitable and wise selection.

These recommended books are graded as follows: (1) Elementary; (2) Intermediate; (3) Advanced.

General View of Catholicism

(1) *Map of Life*, Sheed, F. J.
(1) *Handbook of the Catholic Faith*, Greenwood, John
(1) *I Believe*, Hurley, Wilfred, C.S.P.
(1) *The Catholic Faith Explained*, Trese, Leo
(2) *Creed in Slow Motion*, Knox, Msgr. Ronald
(2) *Faith of Millions*, O'Brien, Rev. John A.
(2) *The Belief of Catholics*, Knox, Msgr. Ronald
(2) *The Spirit of Catholicism*, Adam, Karl
(3) *Theology and Sanity*, Sheed, F. J.
(3) *This is the Faith*, Ripley, Francis

The Church

(1) *Popular History of the Church*, Hughes, Philip
(1) *Pageant of the Popes*, Farrow, John
(2) *The Catholic Church and You*, Grace, William J., S.J.
(3) *One Shepherd and One Flock*, Barres, Oliver

Christ, Our Savior

(1) *Christ, Son of God,* Fouard, Abbe Constant

(2) *Jesus and His Times* (2 vols.), Daniel-Rops, Henri

(2) *Son of God,* Adam, Karl

(2) *The Savior's Life,* Simmons, Gilbert, C.S.P.

(3) *The Christ of Catholicism,* Graham, Dom Aelred, O.S.B.

(3) *Jesus Christ* (2 vols.), Prat, Ferdinand, S.J.

The Mass and the Sacraments

(1) *Mass in Slow Motion,* Knox, Msgr. Ronald

(1) *This is the Mass,* Daniel-Rops, Henri

(2) *Of Sacraments and Sacrifice,* Howell, Clifford, S.J.

(2) *Christian Life and Worship,* Ellard, Gerald, S.J.

(2) *Pardon and Peace,* Wilson, Alfred, C.P.

(3) *The Meaning of the Mass,* Bussard, Paul and Kirsch, Felix

Spiritual Reading

Devotional

(1) *The Bible*

(1) *Introduction to a Devout Life,* St. Francis De Sales
(1) *Autobiography of Little Flower,* St. Thérèse
(2) *Saints for Our Times,* Maynard, Theodore
(2) *Saints for Now,* Luce, Clare Boothe
(2) *Imitation of Christ,* Thomas à Kempis
(3) *The Quiet Light,* De Wohl, Louis

Informative
(1) *Primer of Prayer,* McSorley, Joseph S., C.S.P.
(1) *Fitting God into the Picture,* Oakley, Mary Lewis
(2) *Dark Night of the Soul,* St. John of the Cross
(2) *Peace of Soul,* Sheen, Bishop Fulton J.
(2) *Cana Is Forever,* Doyle, Charles Hugo
(3) *You,* Raymond, Rev. M.

Series of Converts
(1) *Where I Found Christ,* O'Brien, Rev. John A.
(1) *Celestial Homespun,* Burton, Katherine
(2) *Road to Damascus,* O'Brien, Rev. John A.
(2) *Testimony to Grace,* Dulles, Charles A., S.J.
(2) *Fast By the Road,* Moody, John
(3) *Seven Storey Mountain,* Merton, Thomas
(3) *Henry Cardinal Newman,* Moody, John

The Index of Forbidden Books

THE OFFICIAL INDEX is a list of books which present as facts teachings contrary to faith and morals and which Catholics should not read without permission from the bishop, granted directly or indirectly through the parish priest. The purpose of the Index is not to limit freedom but rather to give it, by assuring the reader that, insofar as faith and morals are concerned, the book contains error.

Just as the Food and Drug Act was passed to prevent people from becoming physically poisoned, so censorship, whether by the official Index of the Church or by the local bishop, is used to prevent spiritual poisoning. And, as the stamp of the Government inspectors guarantees the purity, not the tastiness, of the food, so the Imprimatur and Nihil Obstat in a book guarantee only the purity of the official doctrines presented as true.

XIV
FORMS
OF ADDRESS

Forms of Address

The following forms are listed as guides for the use of the laity in addressing officials of the Church.

The Pope:

    Address on envelope: To His Holiness, Pope ....

    Salutation: Your Holiness or Most Holy Father

    Concluding a letter: With filial obedience, I remain, the humble servant of Your Holiness

Cardinals:

    Address on envelope: His Eminence (Christian Name) Cardinal (Surname)

    Salutation: Your Eminence or My Lord Cardinal

    Concluding a letter: I have the honor to be, Your Eminence, Your obedient servant

Archbishops and Bishops:

    Address on envelope: Most Reverend N...... N......

    Salutation: Your Excellency

    Concluding a letter: I have the honor to be, Your Excellency, your obedient subject

Abbots:

Address on envelope: Right Reverend
N...... N...... (adding designated
letters for religious community)

Salutation: Right Reverend Abbot

Concluding a letter: I have the honor to be,
Right Reverend Abbot, Most respectfully yours

Monsignors:

Address on envelope: Rt. (Very) Rev.
Msgr. N...... N......

Salutation: Right Reverend Monsignor or
Very Reverend Monsignor

Concluding a letter: I am, Right (Very)
Reverend Monsignor, Respectfully yours

Priests:

Address on envelope: Rev. N..... N.....
(Add letters of religious community.)

Salutation: Dear Reverend Father or
Reverend and dear Father

Concluding a letter: I am, Reverend
Father, Respectfully yours

Brothers:

Address on envelope: Brother N......

Salutation: Dear Brother N......

Concluding a letter: I am, Respectfully
yours

Sisters or Mothers:

Address on envelope: Sister N...... or Mother N......

Salutation: Dear Sister N...... or Dear Mother N......

Concluding a letter: I am, Respectfully yours

Baptismal Names for Boys

Aaron		Bertrand,	
Abel	July 30	(Bert)	June 30
Abraham	Oct. 9	Blaise	Feb. 3
Adam	May 16	Bonaventure	July 14
Adolph	June 17	Boniface	June 5
Adrian	Sept. 8	Borromeo	Nov. 4
Albert	Nov. 15	Brendan	May 16
Alexander	May 3	Brian	Mar. 22
Alexis	July 17	Bruce,	
Alfred		(Ambrose)	Dec. 7
Allan (Allen)	Jan. 12	Byron	Dec. 3
Aloysius	June 21	Camillus	July 18
Alphonsus,		Cantius	May 31
(Alphonse)	Aug. 2	Canute	Jan. 19
Alvin	Dec. 7	Casimir	Mar. 4
Ambrose	Dec. 7	Casper,	
Anatole	July 3	(Gaspar)	Dec. 29
Andrew	Nov. 30	Cecil	Feb. 1
Angelo	May 5	Charles	Nov. 4
Anselm	Apr. 21	Chester	
Anthony	June 13	Christopher	July 25
Archibald		Clarence	Apr. 25
Arthur	Dec. 11	Claud (Claude)	June 8
Athanasius	May 2	Claus,	
Augustine,		(Nicholas)	Dec. 6
(Augustus)	Aug. 28	Clement	Nov. 23
Barnabas	June 11	Conrad	Nov. 26
Bartholomew	Aug. 24	Constantine	Mar. 11
Basil	June 14	Cornelius	Sept. 16
Bastian,		Cyril	July 7
(Sebastian)	Jan. 20	Damian	Sept. 27
Bede	May 27	Daniel	Sept. 26
Benedict	Mar. 21	Dennis (Denis)	Oct. 9
Bernard	Aug. 20	Dismas	Mar. 25

170

Dominic	Aug. 4	Giovanni,	
Donald	July 15	(John)	Dec. 27
Donat	Aug. 7	Girard,	
Earl	Aug. 26	(Gerard)	Oct. 16
Edgar	July 8	Giuseppe,	
Edmund	Nov. 16	(Joseph)	Mar. 19
Edward	Oct. 13	Godfrey	Nov. 8
Edwin	Oct. 12	Godwin	Apr. 15
Egbert	Apr. 24	Gonzaga	June 21
Elmer	Aug. 25	Gregory	Mar. 12
Emery (Emeric)	Nov. 4	Guido	Sept. 12
Emil	May 28	Gustave	
Emmanuel	July 10	Guy	Sept. 12
Enoch		Hadrian	Sept. 8
Enrico (Henry)	July 15	Harold	Mar. 17
Erasmus	June 2	Harry	July 15
Eric	May 18	Harvey	
Ernest	Nov. 7	Henry	July 15
Eugene	June 2	Herbert	Mar. 20
Eustace	Sept. 20	Herman	Apr. 7
Evelyn	Mar. 14	Hilary	Jan. 14
Fabian	Jan. 20	Hildebrand	May 25
Felix	May 18	Hobart	
Ferdinand	May 30	Howard	
Flavian	Feb. 18	Howell	
Francis	Oct. 4	Hugh	Apr. 29
Frederick,		Humphrey	Mar. 8
(Fred)	July 18	Ignatius	July 31
Gabriel	Mar. 24	Immanuel	July 10
Gaspar	Dec. 29	Isaac	Sept. 26
Geoffrey		Isaias	
George	Apr. 23	Isidore	Apr. 4
Gerald		Jacob	
Gerard	Oct. 16	James	July 25
Gilbert	Feb. 4	Januarius	Sept. 19
Giles	Sept. 1		

Jasper,	Lester
(Gaspar) Dec. 29	Liguori Aug. 2
Jeremias May 1	Linus Sept. 23
Jesse Dec. 29	Louis Aug. 25
Jesus, the name of Our	Loyola July 31
Blessed Lord and	Ludwig Aug. 25
Savior	Luke Oct. 18
Joachim Aug. 16	Martial June 30
Jocelyn Mar. 17	Martin Nov. 12
Job May 10	Matthew Sept. 21
John Dec. 27	Matthias Feb. 24
Jonas	Maurice July 10
Joseph Mar. 19	Melchior
Joyce	Melvin
Jude Oct. 28	Michael Sept. 29
Julian Mar. 8	Modestus June 15
Julius Apr. 12	Moses Sept. 4
Justin Apr. 14	Myron
Justus Nov. 10	Nathaniel Aug. 24
Karl (Charles) Nov. 4	Nicholas Dec. 6
Kasimir,	Nicodemus
(Casimir) Mar. 4	Noah (Noe) May 2
Kaspar,	Norbert June 6
(Gaspar) Dec. 29	Oliver July 11
Kenneth	Orestes Dec. 13
Kent Jan. 14	Orlando May 20
Kevin June 3	Orson Apr. 13
Kieran Sept. 9	Oscar Feb. 3
Kilian July 8	Oswald Aug. 9
Knute (Canute) Jan. 19	Otto July 2
Konrad,	Othello
(Conrad) Nov. 26	Patrick Mar. 17
Lambert Sept. 17	Paul June 29
Lawrence Aug. 10	Peter (Pearce) June 29
Leo Apr. 11	Philip May 1
Leonard Nov. 26	Pius May 5

Plato	Apr. 4	Solomon	Mar. 13
Polycarp	Jan. 26	Stanislaus	Aug. 15
Reginald	Feb. 12	Stephen	Dec. 26
Regius	June 18	Sulpice	Jan. 17
Richard	Apr. 3	Sydney	
Robert	May 13	Sylvester	Dec. 31
Roger	July 7	Terence	Sept. 27
Roland	Nov. 15	Thaddeus	Oct. 28
Romeo	Mar. 4	Theodore	Nov. 9
Ronald		Thomas	Dec. 21
Rudolph	July 27	Timothy	Jan. 24
Rufus	Nov. 21	Urban	May 25
Rupert	Mar. 27	Valentine	Feb. 14
Samson	July 28	Walter	May 11
Samuel		Ward	Aug. 28
Saul		Warren	Feb. 6
Sebastian	Jan. 20	Wenceslaus	Sept. 28
Sergius	Sept. 9	Wilfred	Apr. 29
Sigfried	Feb. 15	William	June 25
Sigismund	May 1	Xavier	Dec. 3
Simeon	Feb. 18	Zachary	Sept. 6
Simon	Oct. 28		

Baptismal Names for Girls

Adelaide	Dec. 16	Blanche	July 5
Adelina		Brenda	May 16
Adella		Bridget	Oct. 8
Adria	Sept. 8	Callista	Sept. 2
Aemilia	May 28	Camelia	Sept. 16
Agatha	Feb. 5	Camilla	July 14
Agnes	Jan. 21	Carmel (Carmela,	
Alberta	Nov. 15	Carmelita, Carmen)	
Alexandra	May 29		July 16
Alexis		Caroline,	
Alfonsa	Aug. 2	(Carol)	No. 4
Alfreda		Catharine (Katherine,	
Alice		Kathy, Kathleen)	
Alisa			Apr. 30
Alma, a title of the		Cecilia	Nov. 22
Blessed Mother		Celeste	Apr. 16
Alverna	Sept. 14	Charlotte	Nov. 4
Amata	June 9	Christina	July 24
Anastasia	Apr. 15	Cynthia	
Andrea	Nov. 30	Clara	Aug. 12
Angela,		Claudia,	
(Angelina)	May 31	(Claudette)	June 8
Anne (Anna)	July 26	Colette	Mar. 6
Annunciata	Mar. 25	Concetta	Dec. 8
Antoinette	June 13	Cordelia	Oct. 27
Aquila	Jan. 23	Deborah	Sept. 1
Benedicta	Mar. 21	Delia (Cordelia)	Oct. 27
Berenice		Denise	Oct. 9
Bernadette	Feb. 18	Desiree	May 23
Bernardine	May 20	Diana	June 10
Bertha	July 4	Dolores	Sept. 15
Betty,		Dominica	Aug. 4
(Elizabeth)	Nov. 5	Dorothy (Dot)	Feb. 6
Beverley	May 7	Dympna	May 15

174

Edith	Sept. 16	Frances,	
Edwarda	Oct. 13	(Fanchette)	Mar. 9
Egberta	Apr. 24	Freda	July 18
Eileen	Aug. 18	Gabriella	Mar. 24
Elaine	Aug. 18	Genevieve	Jan. 3
Eleanor (Eleanora,		Georgia,	
Nora)	Aug. 18	(Georgette)	Feb. 15
Elaine	Aug. 18	Geraldine	Mar. 13
Elizabeth (Bess,		Germaine	June 15
Elisia, Betty)	Nov. 5	Gertrude,	
Ella	Aug. 18	(Trudy)	Nov. 15
Ellen	Aug. 18	Gladys,	
Elma	June 2	(Claudia)	June 8
Eloise (Louise)	Mar. 15	Gloria	
Elsie (Elizabeth)	Nov. 5	Grace	July 5
Elvira	Jan. 25	Greta,	
Emelia (Emily)	June 17	(Margaret)	June 10
Emma	June 29	Hannah (Anne)	July 26
Erma	Oct. 29	Hedwig	Oct. 17
Esperanza	Aug. 1	Helen (Eileen)	Aug. 18
Estelle (Stella)	May 21	Henrietta,	
Esther	July 1	(Hetty)	July 15
Etta	July 15	Hermana,	
Eugenia	Dec. 15	(Hermine)	Apr. 7
Eunice	Oct. 28	Hilda	Nov. 17
Euphemia	Mar. 20	Hildegard	Sept. 17
Eva,		Hirmina	Dec. 24
(Eve, Evelyn)	May 26	Honora	Apr. 12
Fabiola	Dec. 27	Hortense	Jan. 11
Faith	Aug. 1	Ida	Sept. 4
Felicia	Oct. 5	Ignatia	Feb. 1
Ferdinanda	May 30	Ilsa	Aug. 18
Flavia		Imelda	May 12
Flora	Nov. 24	Immaculata	Dec. 8
Florence	Nov. 10	Imogene	Sept. 8
		Inez	Nov. 8

Irene	Oct. 20	Lisa (Elizabeth)	Nov. 5
Isabel (Isabella)	July 8	Lois (Louise)	Mar. 15
Isadora	Apr. 4	Lolita	Sept. 15
Ivanna	Dec. 27	Lora (Laura)	Aug. 10
Ivona (Yvonne)	May 19	Loraine	Oct. 8
Jacintha	Jan. 30	Lorenza	Oct. 8
Jacqueline	July 25	Loretta	Dec. 10
Jane (Janette, Janice,		Lottie	Nov. 4
Johanna, Juanita)		Louise (Lois)	Mar. 15
	Aug. 21	Lucille	Aug. 25
Januaria	Sept. 19	Lucretia	Nov. 23
Jessica		Lucy	Dec. 13
Joan	May 30	Luella	Aug. 25
Jocelyn	Mar. 17	Luisa	Mar. 15
Johanna	Aug. 21	Lydia	Mar. 27
Josepha	Mar. 19	Mabel	Nov. 21
Josephine,		Madalena	July 22
(Josephina)	Mar. 19	Magdalene (Madelene,	
Joyce	July 27	Madeline)	July 22
Juanita	Aug. 21	Madonna	Oct. 11
Judith	Sept. 14	Majella	Oct. 16
Judy		Margaret (Margarita,	
Julia (Juliana,		Maggie, Gretchen,	
Juliette)	May 22	Pearl, Peggy)	June 10
June	Nov. 14	Martha	July 29
Justina	Apr. 14	Mary (Marla, Mae,	
Lamberta	Sept. 17	Marie, Marianna,	
Laura,		Marion, Maureen,	
(Lauretta)	Aug. 10	Marilyn, Molly)	
Laverne	Sept. 17		Sept. 12
Lee	Nov. 5	Matilda	Mar. 14
Lelia	Aug. 11	Maude	July 22
Lena (Helen)	Aug. 18	Mercedes	Sept. 24
Lenora (Helen)	Aug. 18	Mildred	July 13
Leona		Minerva	Oct. 25
Lillian	July 27	Miriam	Sept. 12

Modesta	June 15	Rose (Rosalie)	Aug. 30
Monica	May 4	Ruth	Sept. 1
Myrtle	Aug. 8	Sadie	Dec. 23
Nana	Nov. 22	Salome	June 29
Nancy	July 26	Sarah	Dec. 23
Naomi	July 26	Sharon, a title of the	
Natalie	July 27	Blessed Mother	
Nell	Mar. 31	Sheila	Nov. 22
Norma	Aug. 5	Sophia	Sept. 30
Odilia	Dec. 4	Speranza	Aug. 1
Olga	July 11	Stella	July 10
Olive	June 10	Susanna (Suzanna,	
Olivia		Susan)	Aug. 11
Othilia	Dec. 15	Sylvia	Nov. 3
Patricia	Mar. 17	Teresa (Theresa,	
Paula (Paulina,		Thérèse)	Oct. 15
Paulette)	Jan. 26	Thelma	June 26
Phoebe	Sept. 3	Ursula	Oct. 21
Priscilla	July 8	Valeria	Apr. 28
Ramona	Jan. 23	Vera	Jan. 24
Raymonda	Jan. 23	Veronica	July 12
Rebecca	Jan. 23	Victory	Dec. 23
Regina	Sept. 7	Wilhelmina	June 25
Renata	Mar. 16	Winifred	Nov. 3
Rita	May 22	Yvonne	May 19
Roberta	May 13		

INDEX

A

Abel and his offerings, 16

Ablution, 32

Abstinence, complete or partial, 119f.

Adoration: definition of, 77; object of, 78

Advent, 10; first Sunday of, 10; liturgical color of, 11; season of preparation and penance, 10

"After Pentecost" Season, length of, 11

Alpha and Omega: first and last letter of Greek alphabet, 143 (illustration on page 10)

A M, monogram of Blessed Mother, 144

Amendment, firm purpose of, 51

Anchor, symbol of hope, 146

Angelus, the, 83

Apostles' Creed, 79

Apostolic Blessing, given after anointing, 72

Articles, blessing of, 135

Andrew, feast of St., 10

Ashes, distributed on Ash Wednesday, 112

Asperges: before celebration of sung Mass, 111; symbolic meaning of, 111

B

Bad confession, cause of, 54

Banns of matrimony: explanation of, 69f.; not announced in cases of mixed marriage, 70

Baptism: how to arrange for an infant, 158; two important elements of, 44f.

Baptism in emergency, 46

Baptism of Infants: two to four weeks after birth is maximum period of time for, 45

Baptismal certificates, where to obtain, 47

Baptismal names, 169

Baptismal water, definition and use of, 110f.

Blessed Sacrament: Benediction of the, 87; devotion to, 87

Blessing before Meals, 82

Blessing: of articles, 135; definition of, 132; of homes, 135; nuptial, 133f.; of persons, 132; of places, 135; of the sick, 134; of things, 135; of throats, 134

Blessing, the final, 33

Brown scapular: blessings of God worked by the Church on wearer of, 113; description of, 113; worn by lay person underneath clothing, 113

C

Candle, symbol of Christ, 145

Candles: number of, at different kinds of Masses, 108; used at devotional services, 108; use of, 107f.

Cain and Abel, gift offerings of, 15-16

Charity, an act of, 82

Church, how to enter a, 155; rushing out of, 156

Churching, description of ceremony, 133

Chi and *Rho*, meaning of, 143 (illustration, p. 144)

Circle, symbol of God, 143

Christian name for Baptism, 46

Church Calendar, 10

Collect of the Mass, 24

Communion calls in the home, standard preparations for, 65

Communion of Saints, definition of, 103

Communion of the people, 32

Communion of the priest, 31

Conditional Baptism of a candidate, 44

Confession: arguments against need of, 49; a divine institution, 50; regular hours for, 60; a stumbling block to new converts, 48; what to tell in, 52; when to go to, 62

Confessional: how to use a, 60; standing or sitting in line outside a, 61

Confessor: authority of, to speak in God's name, 50; fear of, 52; God's forgiveness and means of reparation assured through, 50; powers of, to forgive, 48f.

Confirmation: definition of, 67; importance of, to a convert, 67f.

Congregation, not mere spectators at Mass, 19

Consecration of the Mass, 29

Contrition: act of, 80; another version of the act of, 80

Creed, the, 25

Cross, solemn veneration of the, on Good Friday, 129

Crucifix, Prayer before a, 83f.

D

Daily Mass, no obligation to assist at, 37f.

Daily Missals, different kinds of, 34

Devotions: definitions of, 86; no obligation to practice particular, 86

Dismissal, "Go, you are dismissed," 33

Dispensations from laws of fast anad abstinence, 122f.

Divine Praises, 90f.

Domine non sum dignus, "Lord, I am not worthy," 30

Dove, symbol of the Holy Spirit, 139

Doxology, the short, 79

Dragon, symbol of Satan and sin, 140

E

Easter, date of, 11

Easter duty, obligation of, 64

Easter season, length of, 11, 64

Easter water, definition and use of, 110

Epistle of the Mass, 24

Eucharist, a principal fruit (grace) of the Mass, 17

Eucharistic fast, summary of, 122

Evening Prayers, 84

Extreme Unction: how administered, 72; when and to whom administered, 71

Examination of Conscience: prayer before, 55f.; the precepts of the Church in, 59f.; the ten Commandments in, 56-59

F

Faith, act of, 81

Fasting: days of, 120f.; meaning, 120; persons bound by the laws of, 121

Fasting and abstinence: definition of, 118f.; limited to certain days and persons, 119; dispensation from laws of, 122f.; two fruitful ways of fulfilling penance, 118

First Friday devotions, 93

Fish, symbol of Christ, 139

Fixed Feasts, on which we are bound to attend Mass, 12

Feast of St. Andrew, 10

Forty-Hours devotion, 92

G

Gift-giving: perfect visible expression of love, 15; two elements necessary, 16

Gloria, omitted when color of vestments is purple or black, 23

Glorious Mysteries, 99

Godparents: conditions for becoming, 45f.; not necessary for emergency baptism, 47; number of, 45

Good Friday: communion service on, 129; unveiling at solemn veneration of cross on, 129

Gospel of the Mass, 24

Grace, loss of sanctifying, 45

Grace after meals, 82

Green, color of hope, 12

H

Hail, Holy Queen, 84

Hail Mary, the, 79

Halo, meaning of, 145

Hands of priest: outstretched and folded, 21

High Mass, rules for the laity at, 40ff.

High Mass, sung by celebrant and choir, 39

Holy Communion as Viaticum, 71

Holy Communion: how to receive, 154; God gave
   Himself to man in, 17; spiritual value of, 63; the
   surest pledge of life everlasting, 63

Holydays of Obligation; missing Mass on, 35; in the
   United States, 37

Holy Hour, description of, 91f.

Holy oil of the infirm, anointing with, 71

Holy Thursday, on which Holy Communion is distributed morning, noon and night, 128

Holy Saturday, liturgical time for receiving converts into Church, 110f.

Holy Saturday services center around baptism, 130

Holy Water, different uses of, 110

Holy Week, services of, 127

Homes, blessing of, 135

Hope, an act of, 81

Hospitals, facilities for receiving sacraments of Penance and Holy Eucharist in, 66

How to: arrange for a wedding, 157; arrange for
   baptism of a baby, 158; enter a church, 155; have
   a Mass said for your intention, 158; make the
   sign of the cross, 154; receive Holy Communion,
   154; register in one's parish, 157

I

Idolatry, statues do not invite, 115

Indulgence, meaning of, 148; plenary, 149; partial,
   149

Incense: origin, 111; symbolic meaning, 111; uses, 111f.

Indulgences, origin and proper use of, 148

I N R I, inscription on a crucifix, 144 (illustration on page 145)

Intention: how to have a Mass said for your, 158; making a general, 77

Introit, key to the Proper of the Mass, 23

J

Joyful Mysteries, 99

L

Lamb, symbol of Christ, 139

Lamp, sanctuary, use of, 109

Last rites, what is included in, 72

Last Supper, 17

Lavabo, end of Offertory, 27

Leaflet Missal, different for each Sunday, 34f.

Lent, first Sunday of, 11; a season of penance, 11, 126

Liturgical Year, 10

Liturgy of the Church, 10

Lily, symbol of chastity, 142

Low Mass, cold and formal, 18; read by the celebrant, 39; rules for the laity at, 39f.

M

Margaret Mary Alacoque, St., 93

Mass: Christ, the Victim is really present in the, 17; how to assist at, 18; legitimate excuses for missing, 36f.; most perfect act of worship, 14; participation in, 19; outline of the, 21

Masses, types of, 39

Medals as sacramentals, 114

Memento of the Dead, 29

Memento of the Living, 28

Miraculous Medal, meaning, 113

Missal: content of, 34; the Holy Week, 127; rubrics
of the, 34; suggestions for use of, 18-19; used as a
reference, 20

Missing Mass, legitimate excuses for, 36f.

Mixed Marriage, no banns announced in the case of
a, 70; six weeks allowed for arrangement of a, 70

Morning offering, 82

Morning prayers, 84

Mortal sin, conditions necessary, 54f.

Mortal sins must be confessed, 52

Movable feast days, 12

Mysteries of the Rosary: glorious, 99; joyful, 99;
sorrowful, 99

My Sunday Missal, recommended for beginners, 34

N

Novena: definition of, 101; public or private, 102

Novena Prayers, purpose of, 102

Nuptial Blessing, 134

Nuptial Mass, for bride and groom on wedding day,
39; nuptial blessing during, 134

O

Offertory, bringing gifts of bread and wine, 26

Olive branch, emblem of peace, 142 (illustrated on
page 144)

O Salutaris Hostia: English translation of, 88; Latin
text of, 87f.

P

Palms: disposition of, 113; distributed on Palm Sunday, 112f.; symbol of Christ's earthly triumph, 113

Palm Sunday: beginning of Holy Week, 127;
Church blesses and distributes palm on, 128

Pax Domine, "May the Peace of the Lord. . . .," 30

Parish, how to register in one's, 157

Partial indulgence, 149

Pater Noster, "Our Father. . . .," 30

Pelican, symbol of Christ shedding His blood, 140

Penance, when to say your, 62

Places, blessing of, 135

Plenary indulgence, 149; usual conditions for gaining, 150

Pray, time to, 77

Prayer, kinds of, 76

Prayers to be memorized, 78-84

Preface, 27

Preparation, Prayers of, 22

Private prayer, definition of, 76

Prayer before a Crucifix, 83f.

Prayer: definition of, 77; personal and official, 74; private, 76

Prayers: said in common, 75; use and benefit of official, 74

Praying in common, 75; in private, 76

Purple, color of penance and mortification, 11

Q

Quadragesima, period of penance, 11

Quadragesima Sunday, 11

R

Relics: definition of, 116; veneration of, 116

Requiem Mass, said for the dead, 39

Retreats, need for, 151

Rosary: diagram of, 96f.; derivation of word, 95; method of praying the, 91f.; mysteries of, 99; public recitation of, during October, 98

Rose, emblem of beauty and love, 142

Rubrics of the Missal, 34

S

Sacramentals: definition of, 106; purpose and use of, misrepresented, 106; two extremes to be avoided in the use of, 106f.

Sacred Heart: devotion to the, 100; enthronement of the, in the home, 101; public devotion to, during June, 100

Sacrifice of the Mass, man offers perfect gift of love to God in the, 17

St. Christopher medal: carried in automobile, 115; meaning of, 114

Saints: communion of, 103; veneration of, 102f.

Sanctifying Grace, loss of, 45

Sanctuary Lamp: standing or hanging, 109; the sure sign of the Real Presence, 107; use of, 109

Sanctus, 28

Scapular: brown, worn by lay person underneath clothing, 113; shape symbolizes yoke of Christ worn by secular tertiaries, 113; use limited to religious orders, 113

Scapular medal, rules for use of, 115

Septuagesima, a season of penance, 11

Septuagesima Sunday, 11

Serpent, emblem of sin, 140f.

Ship, symbol of Church, 146

Sick, blessing of, 134

Sign of the Cross: how to make the, 154; triple, 154f.

Solemn Mass is a high Mass with added externals, 39

Sorrowful Mysteries, 99

Sorrow: definition of, 51; sincerity of, 51

Spring Equinox, 11

Stations of the Cross: devotion of, during Lent, 94; private devotions of, 94

Stipends: free-will offerings of the poor, 151; not "payment" for spiritual favor, 152

Sunday Mass: obligation of attending, 35f.; stems from divine command to keep holy the Lord's day, 36

Symbols, Christian: animals as, 139ff.; history of, 138; letters and other objects as, 143-146; plants as, 142

Statues do not invite idolatry, 115

T

Tantum Ergo: Latin text of, 88; English translation of, 89

Thanksgiving, act of, 81

Throats, blessing of, 134

Triangle, meaning of, with eye in center, 143 (illustration on page 144)

V

Venial sins, when and how to confess, 53

Vernal Equinox, 11

Vestments, rose-colored, 127

Viaticum, definition of, 71

Votive candles: lighting of, a symbolic act, 109; placed before a shrine or statue, 108f.; use of, is not a sacramental, 108

W

Water: holy, symbol of spiritual purification, 110; uses of, 110

Wedding, how to arrange a, 157

Wedding date, not to conflict with day of fast and abstinence, 69

Wheat and grapes, symbol of the Holy Eucharist, 142 (illustration on page 143)

Worship, perfect way of, 15